GRILL iT WiTH LEVI

101 REGGAE RECIPES FOR SUNSHINE AND SOUL

GRILL iT WiTH LEVI

101 REGGAE RECIPES
FOR SUNSHINE AND SOUL

EBURY
PRESS

1 2 3 4 5 6 7 8 9 10

Published in 2013 by Ebury Press, an imprint of Ebury Publishing

A Random House Group Company

The Random House Group Limited Reg. No. 954009

Addresses for companies within the Random House Group can be found at
www.randomhouse.co.uk

A CIP catalogue record for this book is available from the British Library

The Random House Group Limited supports The Forest Stewardship Council® (FSC®),
the leading international forest certification organisation. Our books carrying the FSC label
are printed on FSC® certified paper. FSC is the only forest certification scheme endorsed
by the leading environmental organisations, including Greenpeace. Our paper procurement
policy can be found at www.randomhouse.co.uk/environment

MIX
Paper from
responsible sources
FSC® C016897

To buy books by your favourite authors and register for offers visit www.randomhouse.co.uk

Design & art direction: Smith & Gilmour
Photography: Martin Poole
Food stylist: Sara Lewis
Props stylist: Tamzin Ferdinando

Printed and bound in the UK by Butler Tanner and Dennis Ltd
ISBN 9780091950804

CONTENTS

INTRODUCTION

I've always wanted to write about barbecue: this book is me! Most of my inspiration, foodwise, has come from its great flavours and its communal feeling of getting together to have fun.

People love to barbecue because you can do it anywhere, anyhow, in any fashion that you want. We do it to celebrate and party, but now this way of cooking has become integrated into everyday eating. You don't have to wait for summer or a special event to dust off the grill. You don't even have to go outdoors! The flavours you associate with barbecue are also delicious if you cook the food under a grill or on a griddle pan in the kitchen. All these recipes are fantastic to eat whether you are indoors or out.

Why do we love to barbecue so much? For a start, there are all the flavours: meat, fish, vegetables and even fruits are all great cooked over smoke and glowing charcoal, and given that special chargrilled flavour, especially with the extra magic of spices and sauces.

And barbecuing is so easy! There's not much in the way of preparation. Then it's straight on out, no pans, and you can cook the food together. It has to be the most relaxing way to entertain – just grill and chill.

In the Caribbean, this style of eating is all about the party and the sharing. On birthdays and other big events there's often a big cookout. You get this fantastic smell from miles away and follow it to the event.

Fire has always been an attraction to humankind and quite often the barbecues in Jamaica are in the darkening, chilling-out time, with music and everyone enjoying cooking and eating. During the day, you can order your barbecue food from a shack on the beach, go for a swim and come back to enjoy some jerk fish or chicken when it's ready and delicious.

Barbecues are best kept simple. Back in the day, the workers in the sugar cane fields would just dig a hole in the ground, light a fire and cook the food on the ashes. From this, barbecue in Jamaica developed into jerk food. Originally, this was about preserving food with spices and long, slow smoking. Nowadays, jerk is defined more by the flavours you put on the food and the taste has spread. It's one of Jamaica's gifts to the world!

The most crucial jerk flavour is allspice, the seed of the beautiful pimento tree. Jamaica is called 'the land of wood and water' and this is one of our national trees. The wood is used for the cooking and the berries squashed up with a mortar and pestle to flavour the food. Another essential is Scotch Bonnet, the national chilli of Jamaica. Other kinds can be used, but they won't give you quite the same heat and authentic flavour. Also into the mix goes fresh ginger, garlic and perhaps some nutmeg, thyme, black pepper and spring onions.

At my barbecues, I always have on hand my Sunshine Kit of these spices and flavours, and you can create your own. One thing's for sure: you couldn't have a bland jerk dish!

Barbecue is a personal way of cooking and everyone has their own style, wherever and whatever they are preparing. For me, it's good to marinate the meat or fish in advance to add another layer of flavour, especially if you don't have the smokiness of an outdoor charcoal barbecue.

As well as chicken and other meats, fish and seafood are great to barbecue and grill. As a boy growing up in the Caribbean, I used to put the fish that I caught straight in the ground, in the hot ashes. These days, I still barbecue a whole fish, leaving the scales on so they act like tin foil to protect the flesh.

You can also roast fish and other foods by wrapping them in foil. It's so easy – there's no fuss at all. Just add anything into the parcel that gives more flavour and makes it more of a meal, whether it's spices and spring onions, or vegetables such as potatoes and carrots. Then add a bit of liquid to keep it fresh and get a bit of steam going on, and perhaps a flavoured spiced butter. Close it up and when the parcel is opened it's all juicy and buttery on the inside.

Another aspect of barbecue and grilling that I love is that the flavours are so vivid and yet it's a really healthy way of cooking that retains the goodness of the food. Meat and fish are cooked so quickly that they are juicy and tender. Vegetables are so full of

flavour that they are part of the main event, not a sideshow, whether it's chargrilled ears of corn, roasted peppers, sweet potatoes, colourful kebabs or salads.

If you're planning a barbecue party, dips and bites are essential, it just gives your friends something delicious to nibble on while the food is cooking. I've given you some of my favourites – all easy to prepare in advance.

And with the main course, I hardly need to mention that sauces add yet more magic to the food. Chutneys, marinades, ketchups (try my banana one on page 198), relishes, mustards, rubs and barbecue sauces are all part of the flavour explosion.

Puddings and drinks are another big part of the action. As well as a selection of sweet foods, including delicious barbecued Caribbean fruits, I've given you some great drinks from the islands – smoothies, shakes and cocktails – that are associated with the sun and the sun-going-downy times.

So gather your friends and family, light the coals or heat up the grill, pour the drinks, get the Caribbean party vibe going and enjoy some fabulocious barbecue, Levi-stylee!

THE PRACTICALS

Barbecuing doesn't need to be difficult or elaborate – after all, it's the original way of cooking and cavemen didn't have a battalion of kit from a hardware store!

Almost anything can be used as a barbecue so long as you can get some flames together and cook over the heat. Even a metal bucket makes a great barbecue. You just put coal on it, then a bit of mesh or sheet of zinc on top. There are just so many ways to grill these days – over coals, on a griddle or using a gas barbecue.

The typical Jamaican barbecue is the oil drum, which we use for jerk and other food. This is big enough for a party and has a lid to help smoke the food properly. Covering the barbecue brings up the temperature to help cook the food quicker. If you don't have a lid, it's even more important to marinate your ingredients to help give them more flavour. You can improvise a lid by using an inverted roasting tin.

Then you need tongs that are long enough to reach into the middle of the barbecue without your hand going over the heat. If you're using skewers, it's best to have ones with long handles so they're easy to pick up. Otherwise a glove that's flexible enough to handle the skewers is really useful.

To light the barbecue, you can buy small paper bags of charcoal that you set fire to, to help ignite the coals. Otherwise, you can scatter pieces of firelighter around heaped coals to help get the fire going, and then spread the coals out. Just make sure the lighters have burnt out by the time you start cooking so they don't spoil the flavour of the food. You must also wait until the flames have died down so you don't burn the food – cook everything over hot, glowing coals.

I also like to use a 'dowser' – a sprayer filled with tasty liquid such as stout ale or barbecue sauce diluted with plenty of water. You spray this onto the coals, rather than the food, and the liquid vaporises to give an extra layer of flavour, especially if you have a lid on the barbecue.

A good barbecue kit should also include a chopper and board to cut up your jerk chicken and other meats; a flat heatproof spatula or fish slice to lift foil parcels and seafood off the grill; and separate trays for raw and cooked food. Make sure chicken and pork are thoroughly cooked, and that raw meat doesn't come into contact with cooked.

If you're cooking on a wooden patio or even on the grass, it can be good to have a fireproof platform to stop any coals from burning the ground. Kids are attracted to flames and it's your duty to make sure they don't get too close. And keep an eye on the flames. You can use your dowser to quieten any flare ups that would burn the food.

1

STARTERS, DiPS AND LITTLE BITES

SOLOMON GUNDY DIP

SERVES 8 AS PART OF A SPREAD OF APPETIZERS

Solomon Gundy is a traditional Jamaican dish, a pâté made with smoked herring that we eat with crackers. This dip is like a souped-up smoked mackerel version of Solomon Gundy. It's very moreish so once you start dipping you won't be able to stop…

For the dip

250g smoked
 mackerel fillets
2 garlic cloves, crushed
20g fresh root ginger,
 peeled and grated
2 tsp grain mustard
1 red chilli, seeded
 and chopped
120ml sour cream
75g cream cheese
2 tbsp freshly chopped
 coriander
juice of ½ lime
salt and pepper

To serve

a dollop of sour cream
1 tbsp freshly chopped
 coriander
1 red chilli, seeded
 and cut into slivers

Remove the skin from the mackerel and discard. Flake the flesh and put it in the food-processor with the remaining dip ingredients. Pulse to a rough purée. Taste for seasoning – you probably won't need to add any more, but just in case.

Scrape into a bowl and garnish with the sour cream, coriander and chilli. Serve with bread, Pitta Chippa Dippas (page 14), crackers or raw vegetables.

LEVI'S SAUCY DIPS WITH PITTA CHIPPA DIPPAS

SERVES 8 AS PART OF A SPREAD OF APPETIZERS

For the mild dip
2 tbsp mayonnaise
4 tbsp Reggae Reggae
  Tomato Ketchup or
  regular tomato ketchup
½ tsp fresh lime juice

For the hot dip
2 tbsp mayonnaise
2 tbsp natural yoghurt
2 tbsp X Hot Reggae Reggae
  Sauce or hot chilli sauce
½ tsp finely grated fresh
  root ginger

For the chilli dip
2 tbsp mayonnaise
4 tbsp Reggae Reggae
  Tomato Ketchup or
  regular tomato ketchup
1 tsp cider vinegar
1 tbsp finely chopped fresh mint
2 tbsp finely chopped spring
  onion, green part only
fresh thyme leaves, for
  sprinkling

For the Pitta Chippa Dippas
8 pitta breads
olive oil, for brushing
1 lime

When you're waiting for the barbecue to heat up, it's good to have something to keep you going. These dips use my sauces and you can make one, two or all three of them – they're all slightly different and super quick to make.

Mix together the ingredients for each of the dips, adding a squeeze of lime or a bit more mayo or sauce according to taste.

Cut each pitta bread in half and lightly brush both sides with oil. Preheat the oven to 200°C/400°F/Gas 6 and warm the bread for 3–5 minutes, or until slightly crisp. If the barbecue is going, cook over the coals for a few minutes, turning once or twice. Break the pittas into pieces and serve in a bowl, ready to be dipped.

MY HOT DEVILLED EGGS

MAKES 24 EGG HALVES

These are a little retro – they were all the rage in the 1960s and 1970s – but they're making a bit of a comeback. They also happen to be delicious and easy. Serve them on a big colourful platter – you need to do it with attitude!

12 large organic eggs
4 heaped tbsp good-quality
  bought mayonnaise
2 garlic cloves, crushed
1 tsp ground cumin
2 tbsp chopped fresh coriander
a good squeeze of lime
2 tsp X Hot Reggae Reggae
  Sauce or hot chilli sauce
salt and pepper

To serve
fresh coriander leaves
1 red chilli, seeded and
  cut into slivers

Boil the eggs for 8 minutes, then run them under cold water and leave to cool. When cool enough to handle, shell the eggs and cut them in half lengthways.

Carefully remove the yolks and put them into a bowl. Add all the other ingredients and mash with a fork so you have a nice smooth mixture. Spoon this into the empty egg whites. Garnish each egg half with a coriander leaf and a chilli sliver and arrange them on a serving platter.

ROAST PEPPER, PEANUT AND CHILLI DIP

SERVES 8

This is based on a Middle Eastern dip called *muhammara*, which is made with roast peppers and walnuts. Peanuts give it that Caribbean flavour.

Preheat the oven to 190°C/375°F/Gas 5. Place the peppers in a small roasting tin, drizzle with some of the oil and season with salt and pepper. Roast for 30–40 minutes, or until completely tender and slightly caramelized at the edges. Set aside.

When cool, transfer the peppers and the roasting tin juices to a food-processor. Add all the remaining ingredients except the oil and whizz to a purée. With the motor running, add the oil in a slow trickle. Taste – you might want more salt or a little more honey or sugar. The mixture should be spicy, sweet and a little sour. Scrape into a bowl, cover and chill until ready to serve.

Serve with raw vegetables, Pitta Chippa Dippas (page 14) or tortilla chips. You can also use this as a sauce – it's fabulocious with pork chops.

2 red or green peppers, halved and seeded
50ml olive oil
100g roasted unsalted peanuts
3 garlic cloves
1 piece of preserved ginger, chopped
½ tsp ground ginger
2 red chilles, seeded and finely chopped
3 tsp ground cumin
juice of 2 limes
2 tbsp clear honey
1 tbsp pomegranate molasses
1 tsp soft dark brown sugar
salt and pepper

CHEESE AND PINEAPPLE BITES

MAKES 12 SKEWERS

Here we have the old cheese-and-pineapple combo – but I've given it an adult makeover with some Parma ham. These skewers are great as they are but if you want to barbecue them, use halloumi cheese instead of the feta. Brush lightly with oil, then cook on both sides until the ham is crisp and the pineapple warmed through. Squeeze over the lime juice at the end.

a small handful of finely
  chopped corainder leaves
¼ Scotch Bonnet, seeded
  and finely chopped
juice of ½ lime
12 x 2–3cm feta cubes
12 x 3cm pineapple cubes
12 thick Parma ham strips
fresh lime juice, to taste

In a small bowl mix the coriander, Scotch Bonnet and lime juice. Toss the feta cubes in the mixture to coat.

Thread a cube of feta on a skewer, followed by a pineapple chunk and then a strip of Parma ham. Repeat to make 12 skewers. Squeeze over a little lime juice and serve.

If you want to make these with halloumi cheese and cook them on the barbie, don't forget to soak the wooden skewers in water for 30 minutes beforehand so they don't catch fire.

CHiLLi TOMATO TOASTS

MAKES 8 TOASTS

This is what I call *ital* – the Rasta term for food that's good, natural and pure. Grill the tomatoes in the kitchen beforehand and eat these as a starter while the barbecue heats up. Or cook them over the coals and enjoy them with the rest of the meal. You could even eat them for a really healthy breakfast.

2 tbsp olive oil, plus extra
    for drizzling
½ Scotch Bonnet, or other
    hot red chilli, seeded and
    finely chopped, plus extra
    for sprinkling
1 tsp fresh thyme leaves,
    plus extra for sprinkling
sea salt flakes
2 ripe beefsteak tomatoes
8 thick slices sourdough
    bread or ciabatta
½ garlic clove

Mix together the oil, chilli, thyme and a little salt. Cut each tomato into 4 thick slices and brush with the seasoned oil. Grill or barbecue the tomato slices on both sides until lightly browned and nice and juicy. Take off the heat and set aside.

Meanwhile, barbecue both sides of the bread, or just the cut side if using ciabatta, until brown. Rub the cooked side of the bread with the cut side of the garlic and drizzle over some oil. Firmly press a tomato slice onto each piece of bread so that it lies flat. Sprinkle with chilli, thyme and salt. Serve hot or warm.

HOT 'N' CHEESY POTATO SKINS

MAKES 8 SKINS

These are really nice to eat with my X Hot Reggae Reggae Sauce or a hot chilli sauce while the barbecue heats up. To make them extra special, serve them with my Avo' Mash (page 94).

4 baking potatoes
vegetable or olive oil,
  for brushing
sea salt flakes
1 tsp fresh thyme leaves
2 spring onions, finely
  chopped
4 tbsp grated Cheddar
Hot or Mild Reggae
  Reggae Sauce or
  chilli sauce, to taste
2 tbsp sour cream

Preheat the oven to 200°C/400°F/Gas 6. Bake the potatoes until soft, about 45 minutes–1 hour. Cut them in half and scoop out the flesh (keep this for another use such as mash), leaving a layer of skin and potato 1.5–2cm thick. Brush inside and out with the oil and sprinkle with salt. Place skin-side up on a baking tray and return to the oven for 15 minutes, turning over halfway through.

Remove the potatoes from the oven; scatter the hollows with the thyme, spring onions and Cheddar. Return to the oven for a couple of minutes, or until the cheese has melted.

Serve warm, topped with hot sauce and a dollop of sour cream, or my Avo' Mash.

COOL GREEN SOUP
SERVES 8

This is a bit like a Spanish gazpacho and a bit like a Mexican avocado soup. It's refreshing and good for you – and gives your guests something to eat while you're getting the barbecue hot.

10 spring onions, trimmed
  and chopped
2 garlic cloves, chopped
2 small cucumbers, about 400g
  in total, peeled and chopped
100g baby spinach leaves
½ romaine lettuce, sliced
2 avocados, flesh chopped
freshly chopped leaves from
  1 small bunch of coriander
1 small green chilli, seeded
  and chopped
125g stale white breadcrumbs
250ml extra-virgin olive oil,
  plus extra to serve
175ml cold water
2½ tbsp sherry vinegar
pinch of caster sugar
juice of 1 lime
4 tbsp sour cream
salt and pepper

Put all the ingredients except 1 tablespoon of the vinegar into a food-processor and whizz to a thick purée. You might have to do this in 2 batches.

Taste for seasoning – it needs plenty of salt and pepper, and perhaps more oil and vinegar. Pour into a serving bowl – because it's ready! Serve chilled, with some ice cubes on top, and pour another generous slug of extra-virgin olive oil over each serving.

2
MEAT

JERK LAMB KEBABS
SERVES 6

The jerk paste here might seem strong but the lamb can take it. Also – and this is an important point so listen up – the spices mellow with the heat. If you're not used to jerk you might think the paste will overwhelm the meat, but trust me – it doesn't.

For the jerk paste

8 spring onions, trimmed and chopped
1 small Scotch Bonnet, seeded and chopped
2 tsp allspice berries
leaves from 3 fresh thyme sprigs, plus extra to serve
2 tsp ground cinnamon
1 tsp grated nutmeg
3 tsp soft dark brown sugar
1½ tsp salt
freshly ground pepper
40ml cider vinegar
2 tbsp groundnut or olive oil
salt and pepper

1kg boned leg of lamb, fat removed, cut into cubes
lime wedges, to serve
Levi Roots Fiery Guava Dipping Sauce, or another hot n fruity sauce, to serve

Put all the jerk paste ingredients in a food-processor or mortar and whizz or pound to a paste. Put the lamb into a large dish, add the paste and turn the lamb over with your hands to make sure it gets nicely coated. Cover with clingfilm and chill overnight if possible, or for a couple of hours if that's all you've got.

Thread the lamb onto metal skewers – or wooden skewers that have been soaked in water for 30 minutes. Barbecue the kebabs for about 7 minutes, turning every so often. You can serve these rare but if you want them more well-done just cook a little longer. Serve on a platter with lime wedges scattered with thyme leaves and a bowl of my dipping sauce. A rice dish is good on the side.

MINTY LAMB AND SPRING ONION KEBABS WITH GARLIC YOGHURT

MAKES 6 KEBABS

These delicious kebabs can be served in lots of ways. Eat them stuffed into pitta bread or a Caribbean-style Roti (page 146), with a dollop of garlic yoghurt. Or simply enjoy the meat on its own with salad and the garlic yoghurt spooned over. They're also great with the Sweet Onion, Tomato and Chilli Sauce (page 196) or the Fruity Scotch Bonnet Salsa (page 192). The long, thin kebabs may look a bit fragile but they firm up nicely as they cook.

For the kebabs
450g lamb mince (not lean mince)
3 spring onions, very finely sliced
1½ tsp ground cumin
½ tsp ground allspice
1 tsp cayenne pepper (optional)
1 tsp fine salt
4 tbsp finely chopped fresh mint

3 tbsp Greek-style yoghurt
½ garlic clove, crushed
pinch of fine salt

To serve
6 pitta breads or rotis
finely shredded lettuce
½ red onion, peeled and
  finely chopped
1 tbsp mixed finely chopped
  fresh mint and coriander

For the kebabs, mix all the ingredients together well and divide into 6 portions. Roll each portion into a long sausage shape. Sink a flat metal skewer into each sausage, firmly mould the meat around the skewer and flatten to form a long kebab about 12cm long, 4cm wide and 2cm thick. Pinch the kebab along its length between your thumb and first finger to create a wavy effect. You can prepare the kebabs well in advance – the morning before an evening barbecue is fine – and leave covered in the fridge.

To make the garlic yoghurt, mix together the yoghurt, garlic and salt. Chill, covered with clingfilm, until ready to serve.

Barbecue the kebabs until nicely browned, turning a couple of times. Warm the pitta breads or rotis on the barbecue (open up the pittas if using) and place some lettuce and onion in the centre. Slide the meat off the skewers and into the bread. Top with a dollop of yoghurt and a scattering of herbs.

LEVI-STYLE TANDOORI LAMB

SERVES 6-8

To butterfly a leg of lamb, you take out the bone and open out the meat. These days you can often buy lamb pre-prepared like this, or you can ask your butcher to do it for you. It's brilliant to cook on a barbecue and you can find a size to suit your numbers; just adjust the cooking time accordingly.

Open out the lamb and use a sharp knife to slash it deeply in the thickest parts. Mix together the yoghurt, tandoori spice mix and allspice in a very shallow, non-metallic dish. Put the lamb into the dish and spread the marinade all over. Cover with clingfilm and chill for several hours, ideally overnight.

Take the meat out of the fridge 1 hour before you want to cook it.

Lift the meat out of the marinade but don't wipe it down – you want a good coating left on. Barbecue the lamb for 10 minutes, then turn it over and give it another 10 minutes. Turn it over once again and cook for 5 minutes more.

The lamb will take about 25 minutes in total to be nice and pink and juicy. (You may need to cut off the thickest part and give this piece another 5–10 minutes.) Leave to rest for 10 minutes in a warm place and then cut into thick slices. Serve scattered with coriander.

1 butterflied leg of lamb, about 900–950g boned weight
150g natural full-fat yoghurt
2 tbsp tandoori spice mix
1 tsp ground allspice
2 tbsp freshly chopped coriander

THYME AND ALLSPICE LAMB CHOPS

SERVES 6

Allspice, nutmeg and thyme are three of the key flavours in Caribbean food. Mixed together for an instant marinade, they really spice up lamb chops.

2 tsp allspice berries
2 tsp fresh thyme leaves
   or 1 tsp dried thyme
½ tsp freshly grated nutmeg
½ tsp sea salt flakes
1 tbsp olive oil
6 lamb chops

Put the allspice, thyme, nutmeg and salt in a mortar or spice grinder and pound or grind to combine. Stir in the oil.

Spread the paste on both sides of the chops. If you can, leave to marinate in the fridge, covered, for a few hours or overnight.

Barbecue the lamb over glowing coals until it's done to your liking and the outside is well brown and crusted with delicious spices.

CARIBBEAN STUFFED SNAGS

SERVES 6

These are brilliant for children – the mustard is very mild when it's cooked. Serve with baked potatoes or put them into finger rolls.

6 thick sausages
6 rashers rindless
  streaky bacon
75g Cheddar, grated
2 tbsp mango chutney
½ apple, peeled, cored
  and grated
2 tsp grain mustard

Place the sausages in a pan of water and bring to the boil. Turn the heat down immediately and simmer for 10 minutes. This will save you the trouble of guessing when the sausages are cooked once they're on the barbie.

Drain the sausages and leave to cool. When you can handle them easily, carefully cut a slit along the length of each one – this is where you'll put the stuffing. Set aside.

Lengthen the bacon rashers – this will stop them shrinking – by placing them on a chopping board and scraping a butter knife along the length of each of one.

To make the stuffing, just mix together the Cheddar, chutney, apple and mustard. Spoon some into the slit you've made in each sausage. Season all over and wrap each sausage in a bacon rasher. Place the stuffed sausages on a hot barbecue and cook for 12 minutes, turning until coloured all over and evenly cooked.

HONEY, CHILLI AND POMEGRANATE-GLAZED LAMB CUTLETS

SERVES 4

This is sweet, sour and pretty as a picture because of the pomegranate seeds. If you can't find pomegranate molasses use lemon juice instead – it's not quite the same, but pomegranate molasses is used for its sourness so lemon juice will work as a substitute.

Mix everything for the marinade together in a shallow dish. Add the cutlets and turn to coat. Cover with clingfilm and chill overnight.

Lift the cutlets out of the marinade and barbecue for 4–6 minutes each side, depending on how you like your lamb.

Place the cutlets on a serving platter and scatter with the coriander and pomegranate seeds. Serve immediately.

For the marinade
120ml olive oil
1½ tbsp clear honey
2 garlic cloves, crushed
1 tsp ground chilli
juice of 1 lemon
2½ tablespoons
   pomegranate molasses
salt and pepper

8 lamb cutlets

To serve
2 tbsp roughly chopped
   coriander
seeds from ½ pomegranate

ISLAND LAMB HOT DOGS
SERVES 6

I like using lamb sausages on the barbecue. They tend to be thinner and easier to cook without burning than thick pork bangers, but use traditional sausages if you like. These are also tasty with My Hot Mustard (page 200).

For the Reggae Reggae Relish
2 tbsp olive oil
2 red onions, peeled and sliced
2 yellow or orange peppers, seeded and finely sliced
2 red peppers, seeded and finely sliced
pinch of salt
1 tbsp Mild Reggae Reggae Sauce or tomato ketchup
2 spring onions, green part only, finely chopped
2 tbsp finely chopped coriander

6 lamb sausages
6 hot dog rolls, buttered

Make the Reggae Reggae Relish in advance. Heat the oil in a frying pan and cook the onions and peppers with a pinch of salt over a medium heat for about 5 minutes, stirring often. Reduce the heat to low and continue to cook, stirring occasionally, until the peppers are soft and the onion cooked, about 15–20 minutes. Stir in the Reggae Reggae Sauce or tomato ketchup, spring onions and coriander.

Ideally make the relish 1 hour or so before the barbecue and leave covered until ready to use. Alternatively, make it the day before and store in the fridge, covered, and return to room temperature before using.

Barbecue the sausages, turning them over, until brown on all sides and cooked through. Place the bangers in the rolls and top with the Reggae Reggae Relish.

SEASONED-UP PEPPER STEAK

SERVES 6-8

Once you know how to barbecue steak it's a real treat that's hard to beat. This recipe uses a big bit of rump that you then cut into slices. If some people like it rare, you can cut slices off for them and cook the rest longer for those who like it more well-done.

2 tbsp allspice berries
2 tbsp black peppercorns
850g piece of rump steak,
   cut crossways, 3cm thick
olive oil, for brushing
½ tsp salt

To serve
buttered rolls (optional)
salad

Put the allspice berries and peppercorns into a mortar or spice grinder and pound or grind to a medium-fine rub.

Brush the steak with oil and press the rub into both sides of the meat. Chill for 2–6 hours so the meat can absorb the flavours, and take out of the fridge 30 minutes before your barbecue. Just before cooking, sprinkle both sides with salt.

Barbecue over a high heat for 4–5 minutes or so on each side, until the outside is brown and the inside pink and juicy. Cook for longer for those who like it well-done. Hold the steak on its side with tongs to crisp-up the fat.

Move the steak to a cooler part of the barbecue, or another warm place, to rest for 10 minutes. Cut the meat open slightly to see if it's done to your liking. If it's too rare, return it to the hot part of the barbecue until it's right. Cut the steak into 1–2cm angled slices and serve in buttered rolls, if you like, with salad.

REGGAE REGGAE BANGERS

MAKES 12 SAUSAGES

My Reggae Reggae Sauce makes a great coating for barbecued sausages, or you can use another good-quality barbecue sauce – the sweetness goes brilliantly with the combination of smoke and meat. You can barbecue raw sausages – ideally chipolatas, which are thinner and cook more quickly – or use my trick here of simmering them a little beforehand so they end up cooked through but not too charred.

12 sausages
100g Mild or X Hot Reggae
  Reggae Sauce or barbecue
  or chilli sauce

Carefully drop the sausages into a pan of boiling water, turn the heat down and simmer for 10 minutes. Drain and pat dry. Brush all over with the sauce.

Barbecue the bangers, turning and basting them often, until nicely brown and crusted with the sweet coating of cooked sauce. Serve as part of a barbecue spread or in buns as Island Lamb Hot Dogs (page 38).

GRIDDLED STEAK WITH THYME, LIME AND CHILLI SALT

SERVES 4

You don't get much simpler barbie food than this. It's just meat and flavoured salt. But what a salt it is! Fresh and tangy! Buy really good steak and enjoy how easy this is. A baked potato and a green salad is all you need on the side.

Put the salt, thyme and zest into a mortar and pound until you have a rough mixture. Add the chilli and pound a little more – you should still be able to see little bits of chilli. Scrape into a bowl. You can make this in the morning for later in the day but don't make it any further ahead than that or the lime will lose its freshness.

Get the barbecue really hot. Rub the steaks all over with a little oil and cook for 3–4 minutes each side, or until done the way you like it. Sprinkle with a little of the flavoured salt and offer the rest on the side.

50g coarse sea salt flakes
leaves from 4 fresh thyme sprigs
grated zest of 2 limes
1 red chilli, seeded and chopped
4 thick sirloin steaks
1 tbsp vegetable or olive oil

MY BEST EVER JERK BURGERS

MAKES 6 BURGERS

When making burgers it's important to use mince with a decent amount of fat. It helps keep them together and makes them nice and juicy. Butter adds another luscious level to burgers and it's my secret ingredient.

For the burgers
750g beef mince
   (not lean mince)
4 tbsp Mild Reggae Reggae
   Sauce or tomato ketchup
75g unsalted butter, softened
1¼ tsp salt

To serve
Little Gem lettuce
   leaves, shredded
mayonnaise
your choice of relishes
   (I've used the Fruity Scotch
   Bonnet Salsa on page 192)
6 burger buns
butter, for spreading

Mix together the burger ingredients well and shape into 6 patties about 3cm thick. Cover with clingfilm and chill, ideally for 1–2 hours.

About 30 minutes before cooking take the burgers out of the fridge. Put the lettuce into a bowl and line up with your mayonnaise and relishes. Cut the buns in half and lightly spread with butter.

Put the burgers on the barbecue using a flat spatula – they will hold together but need careful handling. Cook for 3–5 minutes, then carefully turn them over and cook for 3–5 minutes more, or until browned on the outside and juicy within.

Put the burgers into the buns and let people help themselves to lettuce, mayonnaise and relish.

JERK VENISON WRAPS

MAKES 6 WRAPS

Venison makes a really interesting alternative to beef, especially with this punchy rub. You could also use steak in these great wraps. I like X Hot Reggae Reggae or chilli sauce with these, but you could also go for something fruity like redcurrant jelly.

For the jerk rub
1 tsp ground allspice
1 tsp ground ginger
1 tsp ground cinnamon
1 tsp freshly ground
  black pepper
1 garlic clove, crushed
1 tsp salt
2 tbsp vegetable or olive oil

6 venison steaks,
  ideally 2cm thick
6 tortilla wraps
100g watercress
sauce of your choice

Mix together the ingredients for the jerk rub in a shallow dish. Add the venison steaks and massage in the rub. Cover with clingfilm and chill for at least 1 hour, ideally overnight, so the meat really picks up the flavours.

If chilled for more than a few hours, take the meat out of the fridge 30 minutes before cooking. Barbecue the meat for about 6–10 minutes, turning the steaks over halfway through. Venison is good when it's still pinkish on the inside, but some people might want it more well-done, in which case just cook for longer.

When done, take the steaks off the barbecue and leave to rest for 5 minutes. Meanwhile, lay the wraps flat on the barbecue and warm them through. Cut the steaks crossways into medium-thick slices and place these in the middle of the wraps. Pile on some watercress and dollop with your sauce of choice. Tuck 2 sides of each wrap over the filling and roll up into a neat wrap. Cut this in half at an angle, and serve cut-side up.

STICKY STOUT RIBS

SERVES 6-8

These ribs have a slightly bittersweet edge that makes them really delicious and different. Stout is one of the most popular drinks in Jamaica and makes a brilliant marinade that you can then boil down to a sticky, dark glaze.

2 small racks of pork ribs
2 bay leaves
1 tbsp soy sauce

For the marinade
400ml stout
4 tbsp soft dark brown sugar
2 tbsp Mild or X Hot Reggae Reggae Sauce or barbecue or chilli sauce
2 tbsp cider vinegar
2 garlic cloves, crushed
1 tbsp soy sauce
2 bay leaves

Put the ribs in a large lidded pan and cover with water. Add the bay leaves and soy sauce and bring to the boil. Reduce the heat and simmer with the lid on for 45 minutes–1 hour, depending on the size of the ribs.

Meanwhile, combine the marinade ingredients in a pan. Simmer over a low heat until the sugar has dissolved, then boil for 5 minutes to thicken slightly. Leave to cool and then transfer to a shallow dish.

Drain the ribs, add them to the marinade and turn well to coat. Set aside. As soon as the ribs are cool, cover and chill, ideally overnight, or as long as possible, turning them over every so often.

Lift the ribs out of the marinade 20 minutes before cooking. Reserve about 150ml of the liquid for basting and boil the rest to produce a sticky glaze, taking care that it doesn't burn. Barbecue the ribs for 5 minutes or so on each side, turning and basting with the marinade as you go. Towards the end, give the ribs a couple of licks of the glaze to give them a nice shiny lacquer.

CARIBBEAN JERK PORK RIBS

SERVES 4

These are deliciously sweet and very Caribbean. Make sure you provide plenty of napkins – it's finger lickin' food.

600g rack of pork ribs
½ onion, peeled
1 tsp allspice berries
1 bay leaf
½ tsp black peppercorns
a few parsley stalks

For the jerk paste
8 spring onions, chopped
½ tbsp fresh thyme leaves
1 tsp allspice berries
1 red chilli
1 tsp grated nutmeg
1 tsp ground cinnamon
2 tbsp soft dark brown sugar
3 tbsp soy sauce
1 tbsp cider vinegar
2 tbsp olive oil
salt and pepper

Put the ribs into a large pan and add enough cold water to completely cover. Add the onion, allspice, bay leaf, peppercorns and parsley stalks, and bring to the boil. Immediately turn the heat down to a very gentle simmer and cook for 30 minutes. This pre-cooking helps the ribs stay tender and moist and means your lovely jerk paste won't burn on the barbecue.

While the pork is in the pot, make the paste. Put the spring onions, thyme, allspice and chilli into a mortar and grind as hard as you can. Add the nutmeg, cinnamon, salt and pepper and sugar and grind again. Gradually add the soy sauce, vinegar and oil, grinding and mixing as you do so.

Lift the ribs out of the water, pat dry with kitchen paper and set them in a roasting tin. Spread the jerk paste all over the ribs and place them on the barbecue. Cook for 10 minutes, turning once. Serve immediately.

PORK CHOPS WITH BANANA AND DATE CHUTNEY
SERVES 4

Pork chops are among the best things to cook on the barbecue – the charcoal just does brilliant things to their flavour. You can make this chutney in advance and keep it in the fridge. Pork with banana chutney is a match made in heaven.

For the marinade

2 tbsp olive oil
1 tbsp ground cumin
1 tbsp ground cinnamon
2 tsp ground ginger
salt and pepper

4 thin boneless pork chops,
  about 160g each

For the chutney

1 tbsp groundnut oil
1 onion, peeled and chopped
3 garlic cloves, chopped
2 tsp ground ginger
2 red chillies, seeded
  and chopped
juice of 1 lime
25ml apple juice
50ml cider vinegar
12 dates, stoned and chopped
2 firm bananas, peeled and sliced
40g soft dark brown sugar

Combine all the marinade ingredients in a shallow dish. Add the chops and turn to coat. Cover and marinate in the fridge for a couple of hours.

To make the chutney, heat the oil and cook the onion over a medium heat until soft and golden. Add the garlic, ginger and chillies and cook for another 2 minutes. Add the lime juice, apple juice, vinegar, dates and bananas. Stir to combine and then cook for about 10 minutes, or until the fruit has softened. Add the sugar and stir to help it dissolve. Cook over a gentle heat for a further 7 minutes or so. This is not a long, slow-cooked chutney – it should still taste quite fresh. Check it has a good sweet-sour balance and add more sugar, vinegar or lime juice if you think it needs it. Leave to cool.

Lift the chops out of the marinade and barbecue for 4–5 minutes each side, or until cooked through. Serve with the chutney.

GINGERED-UP PORK BURGERS WITH PINEAPPLE

MAKES 6 BURGERS

Pork makes delicious burgers and the addition of prawns makes a really special difference to the taste and texture.

200g small cooked
   prawns, peeled
5 x 3cm piece of fresh
   root ginger, peeled
   and roughly chopped
2 garlic cloves, roughly
   chopped
1 tbsp snipped chives
2 spring onions, roughly
   chopped
½ Scotch Bonnet,
   seeded and chopped
1 tsp salt
500g minced pork
1 organic egg, lightly
   beaten
olive oil, for brushing

To serve
6 burger buns, buttered
pineapple chunks
sweet chilli sauce
shredded lettuce
mayonnaise

Put the prawns, ginger, garlic, chives, spring onions, Scotch Bonnet and salt in a food-processor. Whizz to a paste, scraping down the sides of the bowl if necessary.

Tip the paste into a large bowl and mix well with the pork and egg. Form the mixture into 6 patties about 10cm in diameter and 2cm thick. Chill for at least 10 minutes.

Brush the patties with oil and barbecue for about 5 minutes on each side, turning once or twice more if necessary so they are cooked and hot all the way through.

Place the burgers in the buns and let people choose to add their own pineapple, chilli sauce, lettuce and mayonnaise.

GLAZED PORK BELLY SLICES
WITH QUICK PICKLED MANGO
SERVES 4

It's very easy to find pork belly slices without the rind in supermarkets and they're terrific value for money. They're also one of the best things to cook on the barbecue as the fat keeps them moist and succulent.

Put the pork in a dish and add the marinade ingredients, mixing well with your hands to coat. Cover and chill overnight. Lift the pork out of the liquid, shake of any excess and pat dry with kitchen paper, wiping off any allspice berries or peppercorns.

For the pickled mango, peel the mango and carefully slice the cheeks from around the stone. Cut the cheeks into neat slices and place in a bowl. Mix the lime juice, chillies, salt and pepper and water together and pour over the mango to completely cover. Set aside while you cook the pork – don't leave it any longer or the mango will go too soft. (If you're making this ahead of time, remove the mangoes from the pickling solution and keep covered until you're ready to serve.)

Barbecue the pork slices, turning, until golden and cooked through, about 14 minutes. Brush the pork with the hot sauce and cook for another minute or so on each side. The pork should be glazed all over and slightly caramelized in places. Serve immediately with pickled mango slices, a green salad and some bread or Rotis (page 146).

8 pork belly slices, rind removed, fat left on

For the marinade
450ml apple juice
50ml dark or light rum
2 tsp dried oregano
10 black peppercorns, bruised
6 allspice berries, crushed

For the pickled mango
1 large mango, slightly unripe
juice of 2 limes
1 red chilli and 1 green chilli, seeded and finely chopped
½ tsp salt
freshly ground black pepper
100ml water

4 tbsp Levi's Hot Reggae Reggae Sauce or chilli sauce, for brushing

3
CHICKEN

ROASTED PINEAPPLE CHICKEN WITH A SWEET CHILLI GLAZE

MAKES 8 SKEWERS

Here are some delicious, rustic skewers just perfect for a party.

For the glaze

2 tbsp Reggae Reggae
  Tomato Ketchup or
  regular tomato ketchup
2 tsp Japanese soy sauce
90ml pineapple juice
4 tbsp ginger syrup (or you
  can use the syrup from
  a jar of stem ginger)
1 tsp soft dark brown sugar
2 tbsp cider vinegar
2 tbsp sweet chilli
  dipping sauce
2 tsp fish sauce

1 pineapple, peeled, cored
  and cut into bite-sized chunks
  (you need 32 chunks in total)
6 skinless, boneless chicken
  thighs, each cut into 3 pieces

Put the glaze ingredients in a small pan and simmer, uncovered, over a low heat for 10 minutes, or until reduced to a syrup. Pour into a non-metallic container until needed. You can do this 1 or 2 days in advance and store covered in the fridge.

Make the skewers at least a couple of hours in advance of cooking. Thread a pineapple piece onto a metal skewer – or a wooden one that you have soaked in water for 30 minutes – followed by a chicken piece. Continue until you have 3 chicken pieces and 4 pineapple pieces on each skewer. Place the skewers in a flat, non-metallic dish and pour over the glaze. Turn a few times to coat and marinate for a couple of hours in the fridge, loosely covered in clingfilm.

Barbecue the skewers on a medium-high heat, basting with the marinade and turning often until the chicken is brown and cooked through – the juices should run clear. You need to pay attention and keep turning the skewers because the sweet glaze can burn. Serve immediately.

BARBECUED CHICKEN FILLETS
WITH MOLASSES SUGAR AND LIME
SERVES 6

6 chicken breasts,
  skin removed
4 tbsp molasses sugar
juice of 4 limes
3 tbsp olive oil
leaves from 3 fresh
  thyme sprigs
salt and pepper

This is so simple and delicious. It's worth going to the trouble of flattening the chicken as it makes cooking easier.

Put the chicken breasts between 2 sheets of greaseproof paper or clingfilm and bash them flat with a rolling pin. If you don't do this you might find that the outside is cooked and dry while the inside is still raw.

Mix the remaining ingredients in a large, shallow dish and add the chicken. Cover with clingfilm and marinate in the fridge for a couple of hours.

Lift the chicken out of the marinade, shaking off the excess. Barbecue for 7 minutes in total, turning and basting with the marinade as it cooks. Serve immediately.

SWEET 'N' SOUR HONEY AND TAMARIND-GLAZED CHICKEN
SERVES 4

Tamarind is a real taste of the Caribbean. We had a tamarind tree growing in the garden of my grandparents' house where I grew up and we used to eat the sour flesh straight from the pod. Mixed with sugar and honey, it makes a Jamaican version of sweet and sour that's great with chunky chicken thighs.

For the glaze
2 tbsp tamarind paste
1 garlic clove, crushed
1 tbsp olive oil
1 tbsp soft light
  brown sugar
2 tbsp honey
1 tbsp soy sauce

8 skinless, boneless
  chicken thighs

Mix together the glaze ingredients in a small pan. Bring to the boil, reduce the heat and simmer for a couple of minutes, or until thickish. Leave to cool.

If you have time, pour the glaze over the chicken and marinate in the fridge for a couple of hours. Thread each thigh onto a metal skewer, or a wooden skewer that has been soaked in water for 30 minutes.

Barbecue the chicken until cooked through, turning and brushing over the glaze once or twice. Serve immediately.

CALYPSO CHICKEN BURGERS
MAKES 6

I got the idea for cooking chicken in foil at the Boston Jerk Festival in Jamaica. Boston is the HQ of barbecue, so where better to learn a trick like this? It means the chicken burger stays together in one piece and is easy to cook and eat.

For the burgers
6 skinless, boneless
   chicken thighs
5 spring onions,
   roughly chopped
2½ tbsp freshly
   chopped coriander
1 tbsp snipped chives
1 tbsp roughly chopped
   fresh root ginger
2 garlic cloves
1 tsp salt
1 organic egg
150g fresh mango,
   cut into small dice

2 courgettes
olive oil, for brushing
6 burger buns, buttered
juice of 1 lime
2 large tomatoes, sliced thickly
1 red onion, peeled and finely
   sliced (optional)
Reggae Reggae Sauce, barbecue
   or chilli sauce (optional)

Put all the burger ingredients except the mango into a food-processor and whizz to a rough paste. Tip into a mixing bowl and carefully stir in the mango. Alternatively, finely chop everything by hand and thoroughly mix together with the egg and then the mango.

Form the mixture into 6 patties. Place each patty on a large rectangle of foil. Fold the foil over and scrunch the edges together to make secure parcels. Put the parcels in the fridge for 1 hour, or overnight if you want to get ahead.

Barbecue the burgers in their foil parcels for 10 minutes. Meanwhile, slice the courgettes into thin lengths, brush with oil and barbecue them alongside the parcels until patched with brown on both sides, and soft and floppy in texture.

Remove the burgers from their foil, brush with oil and barbecue on both sides until lightly browned.

To serve, squeeze a little lime juice over the burgers and place them in the buns with a slice of tomato, slices of courgette, some red onion and a drizzle of sauce, if you like.

HOT GINGER DRUMSTICKS

MAKES 8 DRUMSTICKS

My ginger beer is the secret behind these drummers. They'll certainly give a good beat to any barbecue party!

For the marinade
400ml Levi Roots Fiery Ginger Beer with Lime 'n' Honey or another good-quality fiery ginger beer
3 tbsp ginger syrup (or you can use the syrup from a jar of stem ginger)
juice of 1 lime
2 garlic cloves, finely chopped

8 chicken drumsticks
sea salt flakes, for sprinkling
lime wedges, to serve

Put all the ingredients for the marinade, except the garlic, into a pan. Bring to the boil and simmer for 5 minutes, or until slightly syrupy. Remove from the heat, add the garlic and leave to cool.

Slash the drumsticks about 3 or 4 times in the thickest part, almost through to the bone, on either side. This will help your drummers cook through without burning. Place them in a single layer in a shallow dish and pour over the marinade. Chill, covered, for at least 1 hour, ideally overnight.

If the drummers have been in the fridge for more than a couple of hours, take them out 30 minutes before your barbecue. Lift them out of the marinade and transfer the liquid to a small pan. Boil the marinade for 5 minutes, or until it becomes a nice sticky glaze, stirring to stop it burning.

Barbecue the chicken for 10 minutes, turning often. Brush or spoon the glaze over the chicken and cook for another 5–10 minutes, frequently adding more glaze. The chicken must be cooked all the way through to the bone.

Sprinkle the drummers with salt, pour over the rest of the glaze and serve with cooling lime wedges.

LEVI'S HOMESTYLE JERK CHICKEN WINGS
MAKES 16 WINGS

Chicken is king with these chick-king wings! They'll take you on a flavoursome journey and where you land is up to you! Jerk seasonings are just made for barbecue food. Once you put smoke on ingredients the flavours need to be good and strong so the spices here have lots of oomph. Try using my home-made All-purpose Seasoning (page 189).

For the jerk marinade
4 tsp all-purpose seasoning
2 tsp ground ginger
90ml cider vinegar
1 Scotch Bonnet, with
   seeds, very finely chopped
2 tsp finely grated nutmeg
2 tbsp olive oil

16 chicken wings
lime wedges, to serve

Mix together all the marinade ingredients in a shallow dish and add the chicken wings, turning them to coat really well. Cover and marinate in the fridge, ideally overnight, or for at least 1–2 hours.

Barbecue the chicken wings for about 10 minutes or so, turning them over when they're patched with brown. Serve with cooling lime wedges.

LIME MARMALADE, RUM AND CHILLI POUSSINS

SERVES 4

I love food that's hot and sweet, so this really hits the mark. It's good with the Cucumber, Avocado and Mint Relish (page 194) or the Avo' Mash (page 94).

For the marinade
6 garlic cloves, crushed
1 chilli, seeded and
    finely chopped
1 tbsp fresh thyme leaves
grated zest and juice
    of 4 limes
sea salt flakes
freshly ground black pepper
2 tsp ground allspice
100ml dark or light rum
2 tbsp olive oil

For the glaze
150g lime marmalade
2 red chilies, seeded
    and chopped
2 garlic cloves, crushed
3 tbsp clear honey
juice of 1 lime

4 poussins
salt and pepper

First make the marinade. Pound the garlic, chilli, thyme, lime zest, salt and pepper and allspice together with a mortar and pestle. Add the wet ingredients and combine well. Make slits in the birds in places where they won't be seen – between the legs and the body, for example – and coat well with the marinade. Make sure the insides of the birds are coated as well. Cover with clingfilm and chill for about 6 hours, turning the birds every so often.

Preheat the oven to 180°C/350°F/Gas 4. Lift the poussins out of the marinade and transfer them to a roasting tin. Season with salt and pepper, and roast for 30 minutes. Remove the poussins from the oven and leave them to cool a little – if you put the glaze on while they're hot it will just run off.

Meanwhile, make the glaze by vigorously stirring everything together. You need to use some elbow grease here to break down the marmalade. Spread the glaze all over the birds, inside and out, and barbecue for 10 minutes, turning every so often and brushing with more glaze. Check for doneness – the juices between the legs and body should run clear, with no trace of pink. Brush with a final coat of glaze and serve immediately.

MY AMAZING JAMAICAN GINGER BEER CAN CHICKEN
SERVES 4-6

Wow! Smoky, gingery and sweet, this chicken is the biz. Barbecuing a chicken with a beer can in its bottom is a clever Aussie idea but I've put my own spin on it. Eat this straight off the barbecue – your guests will be fighting each other for it.

For the marinade
500ml Levi Roots Fiery Ginger Beer with Lime 'n' Honey or another good-quality fiery ginger beer
125g X Hot Reggae Reggae Sauce or hot chilli sauce
2cm cube fresh root ginger, peeled and grated
4 garlic cloves, grated
3 red chillies, seeded and chopped
3 tsp dried oregano
3 tbsp soft dark brown sugar
salt and pepper

2kg whole chicken
1 x 300ml can ginger beer

Mix 90ml of the fiery ginger beer in a bowl with all the other marinade ingredients and rub this all over the chicken, inside and out. Cover the bird loosely with foil and marinate for 6–8 hours. Put the chicken into a bowl and pour over the remaining ginger beer (but not the canned stuff). Cover with clingfilm and marinate for 24 hours, turning every so often.

Shake the marinade off the chicken, pat dry with kitchen paper and season with salt and pepper. Open the ginger beer can and place the chicken on top so the can is in the cavity. Place the can and the chicken onto a hot barbecue – one that has a lid – so that the base of the can is on the griddle and the chicken is sitting upright. Be careful. It's a little tricky to balance because the barbecue is hot, but persevere. Close the lid and cook for 40–45 minutes, then check how it's doing. I know it seems quick but I cook a 2kg chicken like this at home. To check for doneness, cut into the chicken between the leg and the body – the juices should run clear, not pink.

Take the chicken off the can and serve immediately. It has such a great flavour that I tend to offer it with salads and bread or baked sweet potato, but no sauces. The flavour is all in the chicken and it would be a shame to mask it.

4
FISH

JERK BARBECUED SALMON STEAKS
WITH MANGO 'CHOP CHOP' SALAD
SERVES 6

For the jerk paste
4 spring onions, trimmed
 and chopped
leaves from 1 small bunch
 of coriander
3 garlic cloves, chopped
½ small Scotch bonnet
1 tsp allspice berries
2 tsp ground cinnamon
3 tsp soft light brown sugar
1½ tsp salt
freshly ground pepper
25ml cider vinegar
2 tbsp groundnut or sunflower oil

6 salmon steaks

For the salad
2 small mangoes
zest of 1 lime
juice of 1 lime
4 garlic cloves, finely chopped
2cm cube fresh root ginger,
 peeled and grated
2 tbsp groundnut oil, plus more
 if needed
2 tsp grain mustard
2 tsp caster sugar, or to taste
1 green chilli, seeded and shredded
1 red chilli, seeded and shredded
leaves from 1 small bunch
 of coriander
about 30 fresh mint leaves
salt and pepper

Wow, this is sizzlin'! Never has salmon tasted so good. You'll be making the salad to go with all sorts of things – it's just as fabulous with chicken and pork. The jerk paste works with other fish too.

Put everything for the jerk paste into a food-processor or mortar and whizz or pound to a purée. Spread this all over the salmon steaks, cover and put in the fridge for a couple of hours.

To make the salad, peel the mangoes and cut the flesh from around the stone. Cut the flesh into slices about 3mm thick and transfer to a bowl. Toss with the lime zest and lime juice.

Pound the garlic and ginger in a mortar. Heat the oil in a frying pan, add the pounded garlic and ginger and gently cook until fragrant. Take the pan off the heat and stir in the mustard. Add this mixture to the mangoes, then gently stir in the sugar, chillies, coriander, mint and salt and pepper. Add a little more oil if you need to moisten it.

Lift the salmon out of the marinade but don't scrape it off. Barbecue the salmon for about 8 minutes on each side, depending on the thickness of the fish. Serve with the mango salad.

SEASONED-UP SALMON
WITH LIME MAYONNAISE
SERVES 6

Salmon is one of the best foods to barbecue because it takes on flavours really well and cooks quickly. I love it with this lime mayonnaise, but it's also great served just with lime wedges to squeeze over. I'm suggesting two fillets here because they're easier to turn over than a single, large piece of fish.

First, mix together the mayonnaise and lime juice and season with salt. Set aside.

To make the spice mix, put all the ingredients except the oil in a spice blender or mortar. Add chilli powder if you like, but this is so full of flavour and fragrance that you don't really need it. Grind the mixture roughly, then add half the oil and mix again. Add enough of the remaining oil to make a nice paste.

Generously brush the salmon with the spice mix on both sides. Place the fish on the barbecue, skin-side down. Turn over after about 5 minutes and then cook for another 3–4 minutes. You want the flesh to be opaque right through. Take the salmon off the barbecue and let it rest for a couple of minutes before cutting it into portions and serving with dollops of the lime mayo.

For the lime mayonnaise
90ml mayonnaise
juice of 1 lime
salt, to taste

For the spice mix
2 garlic cloves, chopped
8cm piece of fresh root
   ginger, peeled and chopped
1 tbsp garam masala
1 tsp salt
chilli powder, to taste (optional)
3–4 tbsp vegetable or olive oil

2 x 400g salmon fillets,
   skin on

BARBECUED SALMON STEAKS
WITH SPICY SHRIMP BUTTER
SERVES 8

Offering simply cooked fish or meat with butter on the side is one of the easiest ways to approach a barbecue. You get the great flavour of the meat or fish and you don't have to do any basting or marinating. Here, salmon steaks are topped with a really interesting spicy prawn butter. If you like British potted shrimps you will love this – it has similar flavours, it's just a bit dubbed-up!

For the butter
100g butter
75g cooked prawns,
  shelled and chopped
1½ tsp ground cayenne
¼ nutmeg, freshly grated
1 tbsp chopped thyme leaves
a good squeeze of lemon
salt and pepper

8 salmon steaks
vegetable or olive oil,
  for brushing

Make the butter first so that it has time to chill. Put the butter into a mortar and pound until completely soft. If you don't have a mortar, mash to softness in a bowl with a wooden spoon. Mix in all the other butter ingredients, making sure they're well combined. Chill until the butter firms up a bit and then, using your hands, form it into a sausage shape. Roll smooth, wrap in greaseproof paper and twist the ends, then chill again. Alternatively, you can freeze the butter if you haven't used frozen prawns.

Season the salmon with salt and pepper, lightly brush with oil and barbecue for about 8 minutes on each side – the exact time will depend on the thickness of the fish. When it's ready, put the salmon on plates, cut off rounds of butter and place them on top of the fish where they will melt into lovely spicy pools. Enjoy.

SCALLOP AND SWEET POTATO KEBABS

MAKES 12 SKEWERS

Here's a chic little eat that you could have as a starter or part of a barbie spread.

1 medium sweet potato, peeled and cut into 3–4cm chunks
6 large or 12 small scallops, corals removed
4 Parma ham slices
2 tbsp olive oil
1 tsp fresh lemon juice
freshly ground black pepper

Soak 12 wooden skewers in water for 30 minutes so they don't catch fire on the barbecue. Steam the sweet potato until tender but still firm – don't overcook. Meanwhile, if the scallops are large, cut them in half to make discs 2–3cm thick. Cut the ham into slices about 4cm wide and 8–10cm long.

Whisk together the lemon juice, oil and plenty of black pepper to make a dressing.

Put one end of a ham strip onto a skewer and then slide on a sweet potato cube. Don't push it all too far down the skewer – this is just a couple of mouthfuls of snack. Thread the ham strip onto the skewer again and then the scallop. Finish by skewering the end of the ham strip. Repeat for all the skewers.

Brush the skewers with the lemony oil and barbecue for a couple of minutes until the ham is crisp, the sweet potato slightly browned and the scallops cooked. Serve hot or warm, drizzled with any remaining lemony oil.

SALMON
BAKED iN NEWSPAPER
wiTH AVOCADO, LiME SALT
AND CORIANDER SAUCE
SERVES 10

Lordamercy! This is just about one of the best dishes in this book. Using newspaper might sound like something a boy scout would do but I think this is the way everyone should cook their salmon. The paper keeps it moist and you end up with the most succulent flesh.

Rub the salmon with oil, inside and out, and season all over. Stuff the fish with half the herbs and spring onions, and some of the lime slices.

Open out the newspaper sheets and lay them on top of each other. Put the salmon in the middle and put the remaining herbs, lime and spring onions on top and underneath it. Wrap the salmon in the newspaper, tie with kitchen string and run the parcel under the cold tap. Soak it well.

Lay the parcel on the barbecue and close the lid. Cook for about 20 minutes on each side, depending on the heat of your barbecue – it should be warm but not so hot that the newspaper catches fire. During cooking, sprinkle the newspaper with water to prevent it catching alight.

RECIPE CONTINUED OVERLEAF

For the fish
1.8kg whole salmon,
   cleaned and scaled
olive oil, for rubbing
4 handfuls of soft herbs such
   as coriander, chervil or parsley
8 spring onions, trimmed
   and chopped
4 limes, sliced
salt and pepper
8 sheets of newspaper

Unwrap the fish and check for doneness.
If it needs to cook a little longer, rewrap the
newspaper, then wrap it in a couple of layers
of foil and return it to the barbecue.

While the salmon is cooking make the sauce.
You can do this in advance if you like but it tastes
fresher the day it's made. Halve and stone the
avocado and cut each half into slices. Peel each
slice and cut the flesh into chunks. Immediately
place the avocado in a bowl and pour over the
lime juice.

Stir the mayonnaise, yoghurt, cream and salt
and pepper together. Mix in the lime zest,
coriander and chillies and then gently stir
in the avocado – be careful not to squash it.
Taste for seasoning. Cover and keep in the
fridge until you're ready to serve.

Serve the fish in its newspaper or present it
on a platter. Most of the skin will come away
from the fish when you unwrap the newspaper.
Serve pieces of the warm salmon with the
sauce spooned over.

For the sauce
1 avocado
zest and juice of 1 lime
200g good-quality bought
    mayonnaise
3 tbsp Greek-style yoghurt
2 tbsp double cream
finely chopped leaves from
    1 small bunch of coriander
1 red chilli, seeded and cut
    into slivers
1 green chilli, seeded
    and cut into slivers
salt and pepper

SUNSHINE TUNA
SERVES 6

Fresh tuna is super easy to cook on a barbecue and this marinade makes me think of Caribbean beach meals, sunny days and cooling dips in the sea.

For the marinade

150ml freshly squeezed
  orange juice
3 tbsp olive oil
¾ tsp ground coriander seeds
1 chilli, finely chopped,
  with or without seeds
  (with seeds will be hotter)
½ small garlic clove
salt, to taste
2 tbsp finely chopped coriander

6 tuna steaks, about 180g each

In a small pan, mix together all the marinade ingredients except the coriander. Bring to the boil, reduce the heat and simmer for a couple of minutes to thicken slightly. Pour into a non-metallic, shallow dish and stir in the coriander. Add the tuna and marinate for 10 minutes, turning the steaks over halfway through.

Lift the tuna out of the marinade, shaking off any excess, and barbecue until just cooked through – the flesh should be opaque and matt rather than shiny. The steaks will take just a couple of minutes on each side. Serve with the remaining marinade poured over.

SOY-GRIDDLED TUNA WITH AVO' MASH
SERVES 4

I bet you think this sounds like an odd combination but believe me it works. The pickled pineapple (page 192) works really well with this too.

For the mash
2 avocados
juice of 2 limes
2 red chillies, seeded
   and chopped
1 garlic clove, crushed
1 tbsp olive oil
½ tbsp soy sauce
salt and pepper

For the tuna
2 tbsp groundnut oil
120ml soy sauce
2 tbsp soft light brown sugar
4 x 180g tuna fillets steaks
juice of 1 lime
salt and pepper

To serve
Pickled pineapple (page 192)

Prepare the avocado just before you want to cook the tuna as it discolours if it sits around for too long. Halve and stone the avocados and scoop out the flesh. Mash with all the other mash ingredients and set aside.

For the tuna, mix the oil with the soy sauce and sugar in a shallow bowl and add the fish, turning the steaks to coat well. Cook them on the barbecue for 2–3 minutes each side, basting with the marinade. This cooking time will give you a moist, slightly raw interior, but cook for 4 minutes each side if you want it done right through. Serve immediately with the mash and some Pickled Pineapple.

BARBECUED MACKEREL WITH BOOZY RAISIN AND MANGO SALSA

SERVES 4

I love mackerel. It's a great barbecue fish because it's so oily and it also goes very well with fruity sauces, which makes it a winner. You can also try the Cucumber, Avocado and Mint Relish (page 194) and the Avocado Mash (page 94) with this.

For the salsa

30g raisins
50ml orange juice
3 tbsp light rum
1 mango
1 red chilli, seeded and very finely chopped
6 spring onions, very finely sliced
2 tbsp finely chopped coriander
1 tbsp finely chopped mint
juice of ½ lime

For the mackerel

4 whole mackerel, cleaned
juice of 2 limes
½ tsp ground ginger
4 fresh thyme sprigs
2 limes, sliced
8 bay leaves
50ml olive oil
salt and pepper

Put the raisins into a small pan with the orange juice and rum and bring to the boil. Take off the heat and leave the raisins to plump up for about 30 minutes. Peel the mango, remove the flesh and cut into small dice. Mix with all the other salsa ingredients, including the raisins and juice. Set aside until you're ready to serve. Don't make it too far in advance as the mango gets soft – a couple of hours before serving is fine.

Slash the mackerel horizontally on each side – don't cut through to the bone – and sprinkle inside and out with half the lime juice and all the ground ginger. Season inside and out and stuff the thyme, lime and bay leaves inside. Leave to sit for 10 minutes or so.

Mix the remaining lime juice with the oil and season. Place each mackerel in the centre of a piece of foil large enough to make a loose parcel, spoon over the seasoned oil and seal the edges. Cook the parcels on the barbecue for about 12 minutes. Open one up to check for doneness – the flesh nearest the bone should be cooked through. If it's not done, wrap it up and put it back on the barbecue for another couple of minutes. Serve with the mango salsa.

JAMAICAN COCONUT-BAKED FISH PARCELS

SERVES 4

Easy. You don't have to do any basting or turning, just make the parcels up and leave them to become delicious.

1 tbsp groundnut oil
1 onion, peeled and finely sliced
1 red pepper and 1 green pepper, seeded and sliced
2 red chillies, seeded and finely sliced
1.5cm cube of fresh root ginger, peeled and grated
2 x 160ml tins coconut cream
juice of 2 limes
2 tbsp soft light brown sugar
4 fish fillets, about 180g each, such as salmon, sea bass, haddock or cod
2 tbsp roughly chopped coriander
salt and pepper

Heat the oil in a frying pan and sauté the onion and peppers until just softening. Add the chilli and ginger and cook for another 2 minutes. Stir in the coconut cream and heat until warmed through, but don't boil. Stir in the lime juice, sugar and salt and pepper. Taste – there should be a nice balance of sweet and tart.

Make 4 double-layer foil packages by cutting out 8 squares of foil big enough to hold 1 fish fillet. Pull the sides of each square up so you are half way to making a parcel and divide the coconut cream mixture between the packages. Set a fish fillet on top and season well. Scrunch the edges of the foil together to make a well-sealed parcel but don't wrap too tightly – the fish needs room to steam.

Set the parcels on the barbecue and cook for about 12 minutes, depending on the type and thickness of the fish. Check for doneness by carefully unwrapping one of the parcels – the fish should be cooked through and no longer look 'glassy'. Serve the fish in their parcels, opening them up to reveal the contents. Sprinkle over the coriander and serve immediately with lime wedges. Rice is particularly good with this dish too.

LEVI'S PARTY SNAPPER
SERVES 6

For the dressing
150ml olive oil
2 tbsp chopped flat-leaf parsley
2 tbsp chopped coriander leaves
2 tbsp chopped mint leaves
½–1 garlic clove, crushed
1 tsp caster sugar
1 tsp Dijon mustard
juice of ½ lime
salt, to taste

1 x 3kg whole Bourgeois or
    2 x 1.5–2kg whole snappers,
    gutted but not scaled
a large handful of mixed
    fresh flat-leaf parsley,
    coriander, mint and
    thyme, roughly chopped
2 spring onions, roughly
    chopped
¼ Scotch Bonnet or other
    red chilli, seeded and
    finely chopped
salt, to taste
vegetable oil, for brushing

Make sure you buy sea snapper and not the freshwater kind for this. But if you really want to push the boat out, get hold of the magnificent red snapper called Bourgeois. This fish is a star – it's magnificent to look at and its dense flesh is a rare treat to eat. I'll never forget the first time I ate Bourgeois. My musician friend Blacker Dread told me there was a fish so good that you didn't need to add anything to it, just a bit of salt. He was right. If you had one fish swimming around your desert island, you'd want it to be Bourgeois. Whatever snapper you're using, get the fishmonger to gut it but leave the scales on. This makes it easier to handle on the barbie.

Whisk all the dressing ingredients together and set aside. You will need to whisk again just before serving to emulsify.

Rinse the inside of the fish to clean out any blood. Mix the herbs, spring onions and Scotch Bonnet together with salt and sprinkle inside the fish. Oil the fish, brushing towards the tail in the same direction to keep the scales intact.

When the flames have died down and the coals are pulsing with heat, place the fish on the barbie. Cook for about 15 minutes, ideally with a lid on, then turn the fish over using a fish slice. Give the fish another 10–15 minutes and turn over again if necessary. You want the flesh to be opaque all the way through.

Remove the fins, peel off the skin and lift the fillets off the bone and onto plates. Season with a little salt, drizzle with the dressing and put a spoonful of the herb mixture from inside the fish on each plate. Magnificent!

JERK PRAWNS
SERVES 4

It doesn't get much easier than this. Marinate prawns, thread them on skewers and cook briefly on the barbecue. Eat. If you're using bamboo or wooden skewers, don't forget to soak them in water for 30 minutes first.

For the jerk marinade
1 tsp freshly ground allspice
2 tsp ground cinnamon
1 tsp grated nutmeg
1 tbsp chopped thyme leaves
3 tsp soft light brown sugar
juice of ½ lime
4 tbsp olive oil
salt and pepper

400g large raw tiger
    prawns, shell on
lime wedges, to serve

Mix together all the ingredients for the marinade in a shallow bowl. Add the prawns and toss them around, making sure they get completely coated. Cover and leave to marinate for 1 hour in the fridge.

Shake the excess marinade off the prawns and thread 5 of them onto each skewer. Set the skewers on the barbecue – one that isn't too hot – and cook for about 1 minute each side. As soon as the prawns turn from grey to pink they're ready. Serve immediately with the lime wedges.

BARBECUED CARIBBEAN PRAWN COCKTAIL

SERVES 6

Prawn cocktail is one of those classic dishes that everyone loves. Here's a Caribbean barbecue version that goes down really well as a starter.

For the cocktail sauce
4 tbsp mayonnaise
2 tbsp natural yoghurt
2 tsp Worcestershire sauce
1 tbsp Reggae Reggae
   Tomato Ketchup or
   regular tomato ketchup
1 tbsp fresh lime juice
½–1 tsp chilli powder,
   or to taste, plus more
   for sprinkling (optional)
salt

30 large raw prawns, shelled
olive oil, for brushing
100g rocket
1 cucumber, cut into 6cm
   batons
3 spring onions, finely sliced
3 tbsp finely chopped coriander
6 lime slices

Mix together the cocktail sauce ingredients, adding chilli powder and salt to suit your taste. Chill until needed. This can be prepared the morning before your barbecue.

Thread the prawns onto 6 metal skewers, or wooden skewers that have been soaked in water for 30 minutes. Brush the prawns with oil and barbecue on both sides until just cooked, turning a couple of times. This should only take 2–4 minutes.

Leave the prawns to cool for 10 minutes. Meanwhile, mix together the rocket, cucumber, spring onions and 2 tablespoons of the coriander. Divide between 6 bowls.

Slide the prawns off the skewers and add 5 to each bowl, followed by a dollop of the cocktail sauce. Make a cut from the peel to the centre of each lime slice and twist it open as a garnish for each bowl. Finish with a scattering of the remaining coriander and, if you like it hot, a final sprinkle of chilli powder.

SALT AND PEPPER PRAWNS

SERVES 4

1 large garlic clove,
 finely chopped
juice of ½ lime
1 tbsp olive oil, plus a
 little more for brushing
¼–½ Scotch Bonnet, seeded
 and finely chopped
3 tbsp finely chopped
 fresh parsley
16 large raw tiger
 prawns, shell on
¼–½ tsp sea salt flakes

Leave the prawn heads on or remove them, according to your taste. Some people think the head is the best part! The shell develops a beautiful taste on the barbecue, if you don't mind a bit of crunch.

To make the dressing, mix together the garlic, lime juice, olive oil, Scotch Bonnet and parsley in a small bowl.

Thread the prawns onto 4 metal skewers or wooden skewers that have been soaked in water for 30 minutes. Push the skewer through the top of each prawn and then through the tail, so that each prawn is on the skewer in a C shape. This makes it easier to turn them over on the barbecue. Brush the prawns with a little oil.

Cook the prawns on the barbecue, turning them over a couple of times, until the flesh is opaque and the shells are nice and roasty pink, about 3–4 minutes.

Whisk the dressing. To serve, remove the prawns from the skewers or serve one skewer per person. Sprinkle with the salt and pour over the dressing.

JERK SQUID

SERVES 2 OR 4 AS A STARTER

Squid is quick and easy to cook on a barbecue and here I've given it a special jerk marinade to make it even tastier. You want the squid body tube and tentacles – ask your fishmonger to prepare it for you, or it's not difficult to do at home. Just pull the tentacles away from the body, remove the guts and the quill, then cut off the beaky part of the head just above the tentacles.

Put all the jerk marinade ingredients into a blender and whizz to a paste. Transfer to a small pan and simmer for a couple of minutes to thicken slightly and take the raw edge off the spices. Transfer to a dish and set aside to cool.

Cut open the squid bodies and place them on a work surface, outside down. Use a sharp knife to make angled slashes in the squid about 2cm apart, cutting one way and then the other to make a crisscross pattern. Toss the squid bodies and tentacles in the marinade and chill, covered, for 1 hour.

Thread each squid body onto 2 parallel metal skewers, or wooden skewers that have been soaked in water for 30 minutes. Barbecue for 2–3 minutes each side, or until the squid is just opaque. Leave the tentacles whole and lay them straight on the barbecue.

Squeeze over some lime and scatter over the coriander. Serve with lime wedges.

For the jerk marinade

3 tsp finely chopped fresh
   root ginger
1 Scotch Bonnet, seeded
   and very finely chopped
2 tsp finely grated nutmeg
½ tsp ground allspice
1½ tsp ground cumin
3 tbsp cider vinegar
2 tbsp olive oil
2 tbsp honey

6 medium squid, 150–170g
   each, gutted and cleaned
a squeeze of lime, plus lime
   wedges, to serve
1–2 tbsp finely chopped
   coriander leaves

5
VEGETABLES

MY MUSHROOM BURGERS
WITH THYME, BLUE CHEESE AND GARLIC

MAKES 6 BURGERS

When I was thinking about veggie burgers, I suddenly realised that a big beautiful mushroom is almost burger-shaped and cooks well on a barbecue. So here's my take on a garlic mushroom-turned-veggie burger.

2 tbsp olive oil
2 tsp fresh thyme leaves
6 large Portobello mushrooms, wiped clean, stalks removed
2 garlic cloves, finely chopped
salt and freshly ground black pepper
100g blue cheese such as Stilton, crumbled

To serve
6 burger buns, buttered
lettuce, shredded
1 red onion, peeled and finely sliced
mango chutney

Mix together the oil and thyme and brush this all over the mushrooms. Put the mushrooms open-side down on the barbecue and cook until they start to brown, about 5–10 minutes. Turn over and cook for another 5 minutes.

Turn the mushrooms over again and put the garlic and more thyme oil in the centre of each one. Lightly season with salt and more heavily with pepper. Sprinkle on the cheese and continue cooking until the cheese has melted and the bottoms of the mushrooms are nicely brown.

Put the cheesey mushrooms into the buns with the lettuce, onion and chutney.

ROASTED SWEET POTATO AND FETA BURGERS

MAKES 6 BURGERS

In Jamaica, we call barbecued food 'roasted' when it's cooked in foil. These burgers are good served in the foil to give them a nice rustic, chunky look. I like oatmeal in my burgers to give them more substance and energy, but they're delicious without.

If you're using oatmeal, lightly toast it in a dry frying pan, stirring often, until lightly brown, about 5 minutes.

Put the sweet potatoes into a pan of water, bring to the boil, then turn down the heat and simmer until tender, about 6 minutes.

Meanwhile, put all the remaining ingredients except the egg, feta and oats, into a mixing bowl and combine well.

Drain the sweet potatoes, mash them with a fork and add them to the mixing bowl along with the egg, then carefully stir in the feta. Form the mixture into 6 patties and press them into the toasted oatmeal (if using). Wrap each patty in a single sheet of foil. These can rest in the fridge for up to 5 hours.

Cook the foil-wrapped burgers on the barbecue for 10 minutes, turning over once. Put a parcel on each plate, open them up and serve, home-stylee.

120g fine oatmeal (optional)
2 sweet potatoes, white fleshed variety if possible, peeled and cut into 6cm cubes
6 spring onions, finely chopped
1 chilli, with seeds, finely chopped
2 garlic cloves, finely chopped
3cm piece of fresh root ginger, peeled and very finely chopped
4 tbsp finely chopped coriander
2 tsp finely ground coriander seeds
1 tbsp soy sauce
1 tsp salt
1 large organic egg
200g feta, crumbled

HALLOUMI WRAPS WITH WATERMELON AND MINT SALSA
SERVES 6

This beautiful, refreshing salsa is so lovely to look at that you'll enjoy preparing this dish as well as eating it! Halloumi is a firm cheese that cooks really well on a barbecue. You can use my Roti wraps for these (page 146) if you like.

For the salsa
1 cucumber
400g peeled watermelon, seeded
1 small red onion, peeled and finely chopped
2 tbsp finely chopped mint leaves
½ Scotch Bonnet or other hot chilli, seeded and finely chopped
juice of ½ lime
¼ tsp salt

2 x 250g halloumi cheese blocks
6 rotis or wraps

Prepare the salsa shortly before you cook the halloumi to keep it nice and fresh. Cut the cucumber in half lengthways and use a teaspoon to scoop out the seeds. Cut the flesh into 1.5cm cubes. Cut the watermelon into similar-sized pieces. Mix the cucumber, watermelon and onion together in a bowl.

Cut the halloumi blocks in half horizontally and cut each piece into slices 2–3cm thick. Some people cook halloumi directly on the barbecue but I prefer to place the slices on a piece of foil first. Cook until slightly oozy, turning over once.

Put the wraps on a work surface and spoon a line of salsa down the middle of each one, leaving any liquid in the bowl. Put a few slices of halloumi on top of the salsa and roll up the wraps. You can serve them cut them in half on an angle, if you like.

SWEET CORN AND PEPPER SKEWERS WITH SWEET CHILLI BUTTER

MAKES 6 SKEWERS

Sweet corn goes all lovely and brown and chewy when you cook it over the coals. These veggie skewers look great and are full of summery flavours.

For the sweet chilli butter
50g unsalted butter, softened
2 tbsp sweet chilli dipping sauce
3 tbsp finely chopped chives
juice of ½ lime
salt

3 sweet corn cobs,
  husks removed
3 red peppers
light olive oil, for brushing

Mix all the ingredients for the chilli butter together, adding salt to taste. Place on a piece of clingfilm and roll up into a small cylinder shape. Chill until ready to use.

Cut each sweet corn cob into 4 pieces – you'll need to use a sharp, heavy knife for this. Slice the peppers in half, remove the seeds and cut each piece into 3.

Thread the sweet corn and peppers onto 6 metal skewers or wooden skewers that have been soaked in water for 30 minutes. I like it in this order: pepper, sweet corn, pepper, sweet corn, pepper. Brush the vegetables with oil and barbecue, turning occasionally, until charred.

Serve the skewers hot with thin slices of the sweet chilli butter dabbed on top.

RASTA ROASTED PEPPER SALAD
WITH SMOKED TOFU
SERVES 6

Red, gold and green are the Rastafarian colours and appear here in the form of three kinds of pepper. Add smoked tofu and a tangy dressing and this makes a fabulocious veggie main course.

To make the dressing, mix together the vinegar and honey and stir to dissolve. Whisk in the oil and stir in the garlic, salt and Scotch Bonnet. Leave to one side.

Cut the peppers in half lengthways, remove the seeds and then cut each piece in half again lengthways. Barbecue the peppers until the skin is brown and the flesh soft and relaxed. When cool enough to handle but still hot, cut each piece of pepper in half and toss in the dressing. Add the tofu and gently stir everything together, adjusting the seasoning if necessary.

1 tsp cider vinegar
1 tsp honey
2 tbsp olive oil
1 garlic clove garlic
salt, to taste
1 Scotch Bonnet, or
   other hot chilli, seeded
   and finely chopped
2 green peppers
2 red peppers
2 yellow peppers
1 x 200g block smoked
   tofu, sliced

BARBECUE-BAKED SWEET POTATOES WITH CHIPOTLE CHILLI BUTTER

SERVES 4

There's something a bit special about a potato cooked on the barbecue. Here the smoky element is ramped up with chillies. This chipotle butter with barbecued steak and pork also works brilliantly.

For the butter
5 dried chipotle chillies
125g butter, slightly softened
2 garlic cloves, crushed

4 sweet potatoes
olive oil, for rubbing
salt, for sprinkling

Put the chillies in a pan and add just enough water to cover. Bring to the boil, turn the heat down and simmer for 15 minutes. Take the pan off the heat, leave to cool and then drain and reserve the liquid. Dry the chillies with kitchen paper and chop as finely as possible. Mix with the butter using a mortar and pestle or a bowl and fork. You can add a little of the cooking liquid too – it's very smoky so only add a little and work it well into the butter. Add the garlic. Chill to firm up, then pat the butter into a sausage shape with your hands. Wrap in greaseproof paper and keep in the fridge or freezer.

Rub the potatoes with oil, sprinkle with salt and wrap them individually in a double layer of foil. Your barbecue coals must be glowing red for this so have them good and ready. Place the potatoes in their foil directly onto the coals. Cook for 15 minutes and then turn them over using tongs. Cook for another 15 minutes. Unwrap and check for doneness – if the potato isn't soft right the way through, rewrap and return it to the coals. If you're cooking on a gas barbecue you can place the wrapped potatoes on the bars and close the lid, but they will take a bit longer to cook. Split each cooked potato down the middle and fill with a few rounds of the cold chipotle butter.

BARBECUED OR GRIDDLED SWEET CORN WITH FLAVOURED BUTTERS
SERVES 6

Apart from meat, this is the thing most people think of when they hear the word barbecue. A barbie isn't a barbie without sweet corn. If your barbecue is busy doing meat you can also cook your corn on a griddle – here I explain how to do it both ways.

You can cook corn on the barbecue in 2 ways. If you only have cobs without leaves, or you're in a hurry, boil the corn in water until slightly soft but not completely tender, about 10 minutes. Brush with oil or butter, season with salt and pepper and set on the bars of the barbecue to finish cooking and get lovely and charred. Turn the cobs every so often. If you don't want to barbecue the corn after boiling, brush with oil or butter and cook on a ridged griddle – preheated until it is almost smoking – turning the corn until charred on all sides. Either way it will take about 5 minutes.

If you buy your corn with the husks on, pull the leaves back – but not right off – so you can see the silky threads. Tug these out and then pull the leaves back, twisting them at the end. Wrap the corn in foil or cook them as they are, burying them in the embers if you're using coals or on the bars if not. They will take about 30–40 minutes to become tender. Don't worry that the leaves turn very black.

To make the butters, mash all the ingredients for each one together and chill. When the butter has firmed up, roll into neat sausage shapes, wrap in greaseproof paper and chill again. Serve the corn hot with rounds of your chosen butter melting over the top of each one. Yum.

6 sweet corn cobs
sunflower or groundnut
    oil, or melted butter
salt and pepper

For the lime and coriander butter
175g butter
4 heaped tbsp finely chopped
    coriander
1 garlic clove, finely chopped
zest and juice of 1 lime
salt and pepper

For the Parmesan butter
175g butter
3 thyme sprigs, leaves only
1 garlic clove, finely chopped
25g grated Parmesan
freshly ground black pepper

For the chilli butter
175g butter
2 garlic cloves, finely chopped
1 medium red chilli seeded
    and chopped
1 tsp cayenne pepper
juice of ½ lime

RED AND GREEN ROASTED VEGETABLES WITH HERBY PARMESAN DRESSING

MAKES 6 SKEWERS

Colour is great on a barbecue, so here's a combination of reds and greens with a tangy, rich dressing that you can serve as a veggie main course or alongside meat or fish. Rather than having orderly skewers, I like to mix things up a bit so they don't all look the same.

For the dressing
1 tbsp fresh lime juice
½ tsp caster sugar
pinch of salt
¼–½ garlic clove, mashed
90ml olive oil
2 tsp Dijon mustard, or to taste
6 tbsp finely grated Parmesan
6 tbsp finely chopped mixed
  fresh herbs (I like basil,
  coriander and chives)

2 red peppers
2 green peppers
2 red onions
3 medium-large courgettes
3 spring onions
12 large cherry tomatoes,
  or 3 tomatoes, quartered
4 tbsp olive oil
1 tsp fresh thyme leaves
pinch of salt

First make the dressing. Mix together the lime juice, sugar, salt and garlic. Whisk in the oil and add the mustard. Stir in the Parmesan and herbs. Taste, adding more salt if necessary.

Now prepare the vegetables. Halve the peppers, remove the stalks and seeds, and cut each half into 4 chunks. Peel the onions and cut 1 into slices about 1½–2cm thick and the other into 6 wedges. Trim the stalks off the courgettes and cut lengthways into slices about 1cm thick. Trim the spring onions, leaving 4cm of green on the end.

Thread all the veg apart from the courgettes onto 6 metal skewers, or wooden skewers that have been soaked in water for 30 minutes. I like to alternate red and green and have 2 different shapes of onion – 1 slice and 1 wedge – on each skewer.

Mix together the oil, thyme and salt and brush this over the kebabs and courgettes. Place the skewers and courgettes on the barbecue, turning over when the veggies are patched with brown.

Serve the skewers and courgette pieces on plates with the dressing spooned over.

6
SIDES,
SALADS AND
BREADS

SUNNY SMILES

SERVES 6

I love butternut squash for its lovely orange colour and great flavour. Luckily, it's also good cooked on the barbecue. Serve this alongside any kind of meat or fish, or as part of a veggie barbecue.

1 medium butternut squash
olive oil, for brushing
juice of 2 limes
mild or hot chilli powder,
  to taste

Some people like to peel squash but I think it's nice to leave the skin on – they are also quite difficult to peel. Cut the squash in half where the bulbous and straight parts meet. Cut the straight part into discs about 2cm thick. Cut the bulbous part in half, scoop out and discard the seeds and cut the flesh into semicircles about 2cm thick.

Steam the squash for 5 minutes, or until tender but not too soft. Brush with oil and barbecue until lightly browned, turning over from time to time. Cut the disks of squash in half and dip the straight sides of the 'smiles' in lime juice and then chilli powder. Leave the semicircular pieces without chilli powder – just roll the curved sides in lime juice.

Serve the smiles on a plate, perhaps with a cooling yoghurt dip or salad.

SMOKIN' POTATO WEDGES

SERVES 6-8

These are fabuloso served with sour cream, dipped in avocado salsa or alongside a lovely juicy burger.

Cut each potato into 6 long wedges. Steam for 8–10 minutes, or until cooked but still firm. Take the steamer off the pan and leave the potatoes to dry for a few minutes.

Brush the wedges with oil and barbecue until patched with brown, turning every so often. You can get nice crisscrosses on the wedges by cooking them on the hot grill then turning them around so the next lot of grill marks are at 45 degrees to the previous ones.

Squeeze over the lime juice and toss well with paprika and salt. If you want the wedges spicy, sprinkle over some chilli powder.

6 large potatoes
olive oil, for brushing
a good squeeze of fresh
   lime juice
2 tsp smoked paprika
1 tsp salt
1 tsp chilli powder (optional)

HOT AND FRUITY CARIBBEAN COLESLAW

SERVES 8

A million miles away from those heavy creamy coleslaws, this is one to wake up your taste buds. It's fruity, hot and even healthy. I could eat this just on its own, it's so delicious. And it's a wonderful contrast to all that hot barbecued meat. Make a big bowlful!

½ Savoy cabbage
½ white cabbage
½ red onion, peeled
½ small mango
3 tsp My Hot Mustard (page 200), or French mustard
100ml cider vinegar
8 tbsp soft light brown sugar
100ml olive oil
salt and pepper
½ tbsp X Hot Reggae Reggae Sauce or hot chilli sauce
2 red chilies, seeded and cut into fine slivers

Remove and discard the cabbage cores and finely shred the leaves. Slice the onion wafer-thin using a mandolin if you have one. Peel the mango and cut the flesh into matchsticks.

Put the mustard, vinegar and sugar in a jam jar. Screw on the lid and give it a good shake. Add the oil, salt, pepper and hot sauce. Shake again then poor into a large serving bowl. Toss in the cabbage, onion, mango and chillies and mix well. Taste for seasoning.

WILD, RED AND BROWN RICE SALAD WITH ROASTED PUMPKIN

SERVES 8

For the dressing
3 tbsp cider vinegar
½ tsp Dijon mustard
2 garlic cloves, crushed
½ tsp soft light brown sugar
180ml extra-virgin olive oil

For the rice
1 tbsp olive oil
1 onion, peeled and
  finely chopped
1 cinnamon stick, halved
5 allspice berries, crushed
½ tsp ground ginger
¼ tsp chilli flakes
500g mixed brown basmati,
  red and wild rice
1 litre light chicken
  or vegetable stock
1 bay leaf
2 tbsp chopped flat-leaf parsley
50g pistachios, chopped

For the pumpkin
750g sweet pumpkin or squash,
  peeled, seeded and cut into
  wedges or chunks
75ml olive oil
2 tablespoons clear honey
3 tablespoons balsamic vinegar

This is especially good late in the summer when you know autumn is on the way. The colours are really something and it's perfect with barbecued pork dishes.

Make the dressing so that it's ready when you need it – just put all the ingredients in a jam jar and give it a good shake.

For the rice, heat the oil in a pan and gently sauté the onion until soft and pale gold. Add the cinnamon, allspice, ginger and chilli and cook for about 1 minute to release the fragrance. Pour in the rice, stir to coat in the oil and then add the chicken stock and bay leaf. Bring to the boil, turn down the heat and briskly simmer until the rice is tender and the stock is absorbed, about 45 minutes. (These types of rice never soften in the way white rice does.) Keep an eye on the liquid to make sure the rice doesn't dry out or burn. When ready, immediately toss with two-thirds of the dressing.

Meanwhile, preheat the oven to 180°C/350°F/Gas 4. Put the pumpkin or squash in a roasting tin. Mix the oil, honey and vinegar together and drizzle over the pumpkin. Roast for about 20 minutes, or until the pumpkin is completely tender and slightly caramelized. Add the pumpkin to the rice salad with the parsley and pistachios. Serve immediately or at room temperature.

HERBY COCONUT RICE WiTH MANGO

SERVES 8-10

You want to put this down on the table and dive right in! It's a very colourful and friendly kind of dish, inspired by elements of the classic Caribbean rice and peas. I've added dried mango which gives it its own USP.

1 x 400ml tin coconut milk
about 300g white long grain rice
1 x 300g tin kidney beans,
    about 175g drained weight
75g dried mango, finely chopped
3 large fresh thyme sprigs
1 Scotch Bonnet or other hot
    red chilli
90–120ml olive oil
2 tbsp cider vinegar
½ tsp sugar
½ tsp salt, plus more to taste
1 large or 2 small red onions,
    peeled and finely chopped
100g roasted cashew nuts or
    Reggae Reggae Peanuts and
    Cashews, roughly chopped
2 tbsp finely chopped fresh
    chives
2 tbsp finely chopped coriander
    leaf and stalk
juice of 1 lime, or to taste

Pour the coconut milk into a medium-large lidded pan. Use the tin to measure out the same quantity of water and add this to the pan, then use the same tin to measure out the rice and add this as well. Stir in the drained beans, mango, thyme and Scotch Bonnet. Cover, bring to the boil, then turn down the heat and cook until the liquid has been absorbed, about 15 minutes. Remove from the heat and leave to steam, covered, for 5 minutes.

Meanwhile, make the dressing. In a large serving dish mix together the oil, vinegar, sugar, salt and onion. Leave to soak and soften a little.

Mix the nuts and chopped herbs into the dressing and then add the rice, removing the chilli and thyme sprigs. Chop the chilli, keeping the seeds if you want it hot, and add it to the dish. Carefully stir, making sure all the rice grains are well coated. Taste and season with lime juice and add more salt, if necessary.

Serve hot or warm. This can be made a day in advance, chilled and reheated just before serving.

HOPPIN' JOHN

SERVES 6–8

This is from the Deep South. Authentic Hoppin' John doesn't include peppers, but many other Southern rice dishes do. This is my version. If you like rice and peas you'll love this. If your butcher can't give you a smoked ham bone, try the supermarket deli counter. Unsmoked will do.

150g dried black eye beans
1 small smoked ham bone
1 onion, peeled and halved
2 fresh thyme sprigs
2 pinches of cayenne pepper
200g long grain rice
2 tbsp corn oil
175g smoked bacon,
   cut into meaty chunks
1 red pepper and ½ green
   pepper, seeded and chopped
1 tbsp Tabasco
salt and pepper

Soak the beans overnight, then rinse and put them into a pan with the ham bone, 1 onion half, the thyme and cayenne. Cover with water, bring to the boil, then turn the heat down to a simmer and cook for about 1 hour, or until the beans are tender.

Drain the beans, retaining the liquid but discarding the onion, ham bone and thyme. Return the beans to the pan. Measure out 350ml of the cooking liquid and add it back to the pan with the rice. Season with salt and pepper and bring to the boil. Immediately cover the pan, turn the heat off and leave the rice to steam for 20 minutes.

While this is happening, heat the oil in a sauté pan and fry the bacon until coloured on all sides. Add the peppers and cook until starting to soften. Chop the remaining onion half, add to the pan and cook until soft and golden. Once the rice is ready, gently stir in the bacon, pepper and onion mixture and the Tabasco. Serve immediately.

QUINOA WITH BLACK BEANS AND CORN

SERVES 8

Quinoa is an ancient grain from South America which is just getting to be better known here. It's very healthy, quite mild in flavour and a bit like couscous. It's very easy to cook and makes a good change from rice.

Put the quinoa into a dry frying pan set over a medium heat and toast for 3 minutes. It should darken a little and smell slightly toasted. Take off the heat and set aside.

Heat the oil in a pan and add the onion. Cook until soft and slightly golden. Add the garlic and chilli and cook for another 2 minutes, then stir through the quinoa and season with salt and pepper. Pour over the stock, stir and bring to the boil. Immediately reduce the heat and cook, covered, on the lowest heat possible for 15 minutes. The quinoa will absorb all the stock and should end up quite dry. Add the beans and corn (drain if using tinned corn). Season and cook until everything is warmed through.

Transfer to a big bowl and gently fork through the spring onions, coriander and lime juice. Check the seasoning and serve.

500g red or white quinoa, or mixed
2 tbsp groundnut oil
1 red onion, peeled and finely chopped
3 garlic cloves, finely chopped
2 red chillies, seeded and cut into slivers
1 litre chicken or vegetable stock, or water
1 x 400g tin black beans, drained and rinsed
200g sweet corn, tinned or frozen
8 spring onions, chopped
3 tbsp roughly chopped coriander
juice of ½ lime
salt and pepper

ROAST PEPPERS WITH AVOCADO, ROMAINE LETTUCE AND RANCH DRESSING
SERVES 8

This salad has a lovely mixture of flavours and textures – sweet, sour, soft and crunchy. Roast the peppers and make the dressing in advance and then assemble just before serving.

2 red peppers,
  halved and seeded
3 tbsp olive oil
1 avocado
juice of 1 lime
2 heads of romaine lettuce
 salt and pepper

For the dressing
100ml buttermilk
  (or natural yoghurt
  mixed with a little milk)
1 tbsp cider vinegar
6 tbsp mayonnaise
2 tsp Dijon mustard
1 tbsp freshly chopped parsley
1 tbsp freshly chopped dill
1½ tsp caster sugar
2 garlic cloves, crushed

Preheat the oven to 190°C/375°F/Gas 5. Place the peppers in a small roasting tin, drizzle with the oil and season with salt and pepper. Roast for 30–40 minutes, or until completely tender and slightly caramelized at the edges. Allow to cool and then cut into strips, lengthways, as neatly as you can. You can peel off the skins if you like.

Halve and stone the avocado and cut into slices, lengthways. Peel the skin off each slice, immediately place in a bowl and squeeze over the lime juice. Season with salt and pepper. Cut the lettuce leaves off the hard base and either cut or tear them into broad strips.

Mix all the ingredients for the dressing together and just before serving toss with the lettuce, avocado and peppers.

SALAD OF CHILLI AND HONEY PEACHES, LEAVES AND PECANS
SERVES 6

One to get ready before your guests arrive (though don't dress it until the last minute). This is good as either a starter, or a side dish to eat with pork.

15g butter
80g pecan halves
4 tsp soft dark brown sugar
4 ripe peaches
2 tbsp olive oil
1 tbsp X Hot Reggae Reggae
   Sauce or hot chilli sauce
4 tsp caster sugar
3½ tbsp balsamic vinegar
150g watercress

For the dressing
1 tbsp white wine vinegar
1 red chilli, seeded and sliced
1 tsp clear honey
½ tsp grain mustard
70ml extra-virgin olive oil
salt and pepper

Melt the butter in a small frying pan and add the pecans. Sauté for about 30 seconds, then add the brown sugar and stir while it melts and coats the nuts. Keep cooking until you can smell that the sugar has caramelized – it only takes seconds so be careful not to let it burn. Tip the pecans onto a plate and leave to cool.

Make the dressing by mixing together all the dressing ingredients except the oil. Gradually whisk in the oil. Set aside.

Halve and stone the peaches, then cut each half into 3 thick slices. Heat a ridged griddle pan until very hot. While it is heating up place the peaches in a bowl with the oil and hot sauce and turn them over with your hands to coat well. Griddle the peaches for about 40 seconds on each side, then sprinkle over the caster sugar and add the balsamic vinegar. The vinegar will splutter and reduce instantly. Transfer to a plate while you assemble the salad.

Put the watercress and pecans into a shallow bowl and toss with most of the dressing. Scatter the peaches among the leaves, drizzle with the remaining dressing and serve.

CARIBBEAN CUCUMBER AND YOGHURT SALAD
SERVES 6

I love cooling cucumber and this simple salad is delicious with all grilled meats and fish.

300ml natural yoghurt
3 tbsp finely chopped fresh
  mint, plus ½ tbsp extra
  for sprinkling
3 tbsp finely chopped
  fresh coriander
4 spring onions, finely chopped
1 garlic clove, mashed
½ tsp salt, plus more to taste
¼ tsp ground allspice
1 cucumber

Put the yoghurt into a bowl and stir in all the remaining ingredients except the cucumber. You can do this well in advance – the night before is fine.

Shortly before eating, coarsely grate the cucumber and stir it into the yoghurt mixture. Check the seasoning, adding more salt to taste, and leave in the fridge, covered, until ready to eat. Sprinkle over the extra chopped mint and serve.

COOL GREEN LEAF AND AVO' SALAD WITH COCONUT DRESSING

SERVES 6

This is a little South-East Asian in influence. I love salad dressings from this part of the world – a good mixture of sweet, salty and sour. This works very well with barbecued meat and fish.

To make the dressing, mix the cornflour with a couple of tablespoons of the coconut milk. Put the remaining coconut milk and the sugar into a pan and bring to just under the boil. Add the cornflour mixture and stir well. Turn the heat down and simmer, stirring from time to time until it thickens, about 5 minutes. Leave to cool. The dressing should be as thick as single cream once it has cooled completely. Mix in the remaining dressing ingredients and set aside.

For the salad, halve the cucumber lengthways and scoop out the seeds with a teaspoon. Cut the flesh into 7cm batons. Cook the peas and beans in boiling water until tender. Rinse immediately in cold water to set their bright green colour and cool them a little.

Put the leaves, herbs, cucumber, peas and beans into a broad shallow bowl. Halve, stone and slice the avocados and then peel the skin from each slice. Add to the bowl and gently toss with the oil, lime juice and salt and pepper – this gives everything a lovely gloss. Gently toss with the dressing and serve immediately.

For the dressing
½ tsp cornflour
125ml coconut milk
1 tsp caster sugar
2 tsp fish sauce
juice of ½ lime
1 medium red chilli, seeded
 and sliced as fine as possible

For the salad
½ large cucumber
150g fresh peas, podded weight
150g mangetout, French
 beans or sugar snap peas,
 or a mixture
200g mixed leaves and herbs
 such as baby spinach, Little
 Gem, coriander and mint
2 avocados
2 tbsp groundnut oil
juice of ½ lime
salt and pepper

REGGAE REGGAE HERBELICIOUS POTATO SALAD

SERVES 6

Potato salad is a classic barbecue dish-on-the-side, traditionally made with mayonnaise. This a different take, using a touch of hot sauce.

750g new potatoes
1 tsp salt
2 mint sprigs

For the Reggae Reggae dressing
1½ tbsp lime juice
1 tsp honey
3 tbsp olive oil
2 tbsp X Hot Reggae Reggae
   Sauce or hot chilli sauce
3 spring onions, finely sliced
2 tbsp finely chopped coriander
   leaf and stalk
2 tbsp finely chopped
   mint leaves

Cut the potatoes in half and put them into a pan, cover with water and add the salt and mint. Bring to the boil, turn the heat down and simmer until the potatoes are only just tender; you don't want them mushy.

While the potatoes are cooking, make the Reggae Reggae dressing. Put the lime juice and honey in a large serving bowl and stir to dissolve. Add the oil and hot sauce and whisk together. Stir in the spring onions and herbs.

When the potatoes are cooked, drain and add them to the bowl with the dressing, carefully stir and then leave to cool slightly. Taste and adjust the seasoning if necessary. Eat warm or cold.

TOMATO, MELON AND CUCUMBER SALAD WITH MINT AND CHILLI DRESSING

SERVES 6

Melon. It might sound like an odd thing to serve in a savoury salad but this works really well. You can turn it into a salsa by chopping the cucumber and fruit into small dice and adding some more chopped red chilli. Be sure to include watermelon in the melon mix.

For the dressing
1¾ tbsp white wine vinegar
2 tbsp groundnut oil
4 tbsp olive oil
18 fresh mint leaves
½ tsp Dijon mustard
2 tsp caster sugar
1 red chilli, seeded
   and chopped
salt and pepper

350g flavourful tomatoes,
   preferably cherry tomatoes
300g mixed melon flesh,
   (such as honeydew,
   charentais, ogen and
   watermelon), seeded
   and cubed
1 small or ½ large cucumber

To make the dressing, simply whizz everything except the chilli in a blender. Add the chilli and check the seasoning – this is a sweet-sour dressing so you need to get the balance right.

Cut the tomatoes into quarters or eighths, depending on their size, or halve them if using cherry tomatoes. Put them in a bowl with the melon cubes.

Halve the cucumber lengthways and scoop the seeds out with a teaspoon. Cut each half into slices about 3mm thick. Combine the tomatoes, cucumber and melon, toss with the dressing and serve.

MANGO, CARROT, CUCUMBER, LIME AND MINT SALAD

SERVES 6

½ small cucumber, peeled
1 large carrot, peeled
½ mango
leaves from 1 small
  bunch of mint, torn
juice of 2 limes
2 tbsp olive oil
1 red chilli, seeded
  and finely chopped
1 tsp caster sugar

Fresh, sweet and tangy, this is fabulous with fish (yes, really) or chicken.

Cut the cucumber in half lengthways and remove the seeds with a teaspoon. Using a vegetable peeler, shave the carrot and cucumber into ribbons. Peel the mango, slice the flesh from around the stone and cut into matchsticks. Throw these in a bowl with the carrot, cucumber and mint.

Combine the rest of the ingredients to make a dressing, stirring well to dissolve the sugar, and toss everything together. You need to make this no more than 30 minutes before you want to serve or it will become too soft.

ROTIS
MAKES 4

I didn't really grow up with rotis – they're more of a Trinidadian thing – but they're very useful at barbecues for wrapping things. Cook them indoors in a frying pan or heat an upturned metal wok (not one with a wooden handle please!) on the barbecue and use the dome as a griddle.

225g plain flour, plus
   extra for dusting
2 tsp baking powder
1 tsp salt
40g cold butter, cubed
1 tsp caster sugar
150ml warm water
about 2 tbsp groundnut oil

Put the flour, baking powder and salt in a bowl and rub in the butter. Add the sugar and rub that in too. Gradually add as much water as you need to turn the mixture into soft dough. Knead for a few minutes and then separate into 4 pieces.

On a lightly floured surface, roll each piece of dough into a ball and then flatten into a circle about 23cm across. Brush each circle with a little oil, then fold it and fold it again to form a triangle. Now roll each piece into a circle again.

Heat about ¼ tablespoon oil in a frying pan and cook a roti for 3–4 minutes, turning frequently. Repeat. If you want to do it on the barbecue, set an upturned metal wok on the bars and allow it to heat up. Lightly brush each roti with oil and cook on the dome of the wok, turning frequently.

FESTIVALS

Festivals are a Caribbean thing: fried bread, a bit like a doughnut, eaten with jerk food. Some versions are very sweet and contain lots of sugar and cinnamon, but these ones are savoury. You can use plain flour without the cornmeal if you like (just increase the quantity of plain flour) but the cornmeal gives them a lovely colour and texture.

Sieve all the dry ingredients into a large bowl. Add enough of the water to bring the mixture together into a ball. Knead for about 4 minutes, then separate the dough into 12 balls. Form each ball into a narrow oval about 10–13cm long and set them on a lightly floured surface.

When you've shaped all the festivals, heat enough oil in a large pan to deep-fry them. The oil swells up a bit when you add the festivals so don't overfill the pan with oil and make sure the pan's large enough. Fry about 3 at a time, turning them over, for 6–8 minutes. Drain on a double layer of kitchen paper and serve immediately.

125g plain flour
125g cornmeal
1 tsp baking powder
1 tbsp soft light
   brown sugar
½ tsp salt
about 250ml water
sunflower or groundnut
   oil, for deep frying

7
PUDDINGs

PINEAPPLE WiTH A RUM, NUTMEG AND HONEY GLAZE

MAKES 8 SEGMENTS

For the glaze
4 tbsp dark rum
4 tbsp honey
4 tbsp orange juice
a good grating of nutmeg

1 pineapple
lime wedges, to serve

Cooked on a barbecue, pineapple gives out its sweet juices and tastes even better than it does raw. Add a rum and honey glaze and you've got a tiptop end to your meal.

Mix together the glaze ingredients, tasting to get the right amount of nutmeg.

Slice off the top and bottom of the pineapple, cut it lengthways into quarters and then remove the core. Cut each quarter in half lengthways so you have 8 unpeeled segments.

Brush each segment with the glaze and barbecue over a medium-low heat, cooking each side a couple of times and brushing with the glaze. The pineapple is ready when the pieces are patched with brown and the flesh is nice and juicy.

Serve with lime wedges and eat with your hands – the best way!

ROASTED DEMERARA SUGAR PEARS

SERVES 6

Ginger, pears and lime make a great combo, especially when mixed with butter and melting demerara sugar. You can use under-ripe pears for this dish, which is useful 'cos that's the way you usually find them in the shops!

6 firm pears
30g unsalted butter, cubed
3 tbsp demerara sugar
2 preserved stem ginger bulbs,
  cut into small pieces, plus
  1 tbsp syrup from the jar
juice of 1 lime
cream or ice cream, to serve

Cut 2 large pieces of foil of double thickness. Peel, core and quarter the pears, cutting off the stalks. Place 12 quarters in the centre of each piece of foil and dot with the butter. Sprinkle over the sugar, stem ginger, ginger syrup and lime juice.

Seal the parcels and put them on the barbecue. Cook for 20–30 minutes, or until the juices are sizzling and the fruit is nice and hot. Serve with cream or ice cream.

ROAST BANANA AND BROWN SUGAR FOOL

SERVES 8

Oh this is delicious! And such a perfect way to use up bananas that are really too soft to eat. It's a very easy recipe but don't underestimate how tasty it is. You'll be stealing spoonfuls of it from the fridge before you serve it …

5 ripe bananas
juice and grated zest of 2 limes
50g soft dark brown sugar,
  plus more to taste
50–100ml dark rum
250ml double cream
4 heaped tbsp
  Greek-style yoghurt

Preheat the oven to 180°C/350°F/Gas 4. Peel the bananas and put them into an ovenproof dish with the lime juice and zest. Sprinkle over the sugar and add a good slug of rum to moisten. Roast for about 1 hour. This sounds like a long time to cook the bananas but it concentrates their flavour. They should be completely tender and golden brown when done. Leave to cool in the cooking juices.

Whip the cream in a bowl and stir in the yoghurt. Mash the banana into the roasting juices. Combine the cream and the banana and taste for sweetness – you may want some more sugar. Add more rum to taste but be careful not to make the mixture too runny. Cover and chill until ready to serve. The mixture will firm up a little in the fridge.

GRIDDLED MANGO CHEEKS
WITH BARBADOS CREAM
SERVES 8

I'd say this is probably the easiest barbecue pud recipe. Do the cream the day before. Get somebody else to barbie the mango. Serve.

For the Barbados cream, whip the cream until it holds its shape but isn't stiff. Stir in the yoghurt. Transfer to a wide bowl – you want a large surface area – and sprinkle the sugar on top. You will immediately see the sugar start to melt and form a lovely crust. Chill for about 12 hours before serving, or make it the day before.

Cut the mango 'cheeks' from either side of the stone. Brush with maple syrup and cook on a hot griddle pan until nicely charred and quite soft. You can also do it on the barbecue – just set the cheeks on the bars.

Serve each person a mango cheek – you can drizzle a little rum over each one, or offer wedges of lime to squeeze over the mango flesh – with the Barbados cream.

For the Barbados cream
200ml double cream
300g Greek-style yoghurt
75g muscovado sugar

4 mangoes
4 tsp maple syrup
white rum, for drizzling
  (optional)
lime wedges, to serve
  (optional)

BROWN SUGAR, LIME AND VANILLA APRICOTS BAKED IN PARCELS

SERVES 4

Apricots develop a gorgeous flavour when they're heated, making them one of the best fruits to bake on the barbie. Even those hard tasteless ones we often get in Britain become delicious with this treatment. And it's no hassle. All you have to do is bake the parcels.

12 apricots, halved and stoned
   (slightly unripe are best)
4 tbsp soft dark brown sugar
2–3 tsp vanilla extract
juice of 2 limes
20g butter
vanilla ice cream, to serve

Divide the apricots between 4 squares of tin foil, setting them in the centre. Divide the other ingredients except the ice cream between each square and pull the foil up round the fruit, scrunching the edges together. Wrap another layer of foil around each parcel to seal.

Set the parcels on the barbecue and cook for 20 minutes. The apricots should soften in this time but have a little peek to check. If the fruit is tender, take the parcels off the barbecue and serve the apricots in the foil, topped with a big scoop of vanilla ice cream. If they're not quite ready, cook them for a little longer.

ROASTED TREACLE TOFFEE BANANAS

MAKES 6

Cooking bananas on a barbecue is super easy. You just wrap them in foil, place them on the grill when there's space, and leave them there, turning once or twice, until you're ready for pudding. Enjoy the lovely, gooey, sweet, brown-sugary centre with some cream or ice cream.

50g unsalted butter, softened
50g dark muscovado sugar
1 tsp vanilla extract
6 bananas
clotted cream or vanilla ice
  cream, to serve

Mix together the butter, sugar and vanilla extract. Cut into each banana through the skin, almost down to the bottom of the fruit.

Divide the sugary vanilla butter between the bananas, pushing it down into the cut and spreading it out. Close up the fruit and wrap in a layer of foil. Barbecue, turning occasionally, until the fruit has softened and the butter and sugar have melted. Allow about 20 minutes, but you can leave them there for as long as you need to if the fire isn't too hot.

Serve with clotted cream or vanilla ice cream.

BARBIED BANANA
WITH PASSION FRUIT CREAM
SERVES 6

This is another take on barbecued bananas – this time their sweet fudginess is slightly cut with passion fruit. I know passion fruit can be expensive but you only need four to make the cream. If you can get them cheaply, buy more and spoon some pulp on top for extra tang.

25g butter, softened
25g soft light brown sugar
6 bananas
4 passion fruit, or more
  if your budget allows
300ml double or
  whipping cream
3 tbsp icing sugar

Mix together the butter and sugar. Cut along the skin on the inside of each banana, almost right through the flesh. Divide the sugary butter between the bananas, pushing the mixture into the cuts. Close up the fruit and wrap each banana in foil. Place on a warm barbecue and turn occasionally until the bananas are soft and the butter and sugar melted. Allow about 20 minutes, but you can leave them there for as long as you need to if the fire isn't too hot.

While the bananas are cooking, scoop out the pulp of 4 passion fruit and push it through a sieve. Discard half the seeds and return the remaining seeds back to the pulp.

Beat the cream until it just holds its shape, and then add the passion fruit pulp and icing sugar. Open your banana parcels, gently ease open the banana skins and spoon the passion fruit cream onto the flesh. If you do have more passion fruit pulp, spoon it on top of the cream to make your bananas look gorgeous.

GRAPEFRUIT AND ANGOSTURA BITTERS SORBET

SERVES 8

This is a good grown-up pudding with a nice bitter tang – you can also make it way in advance.

Put the water and sugar into a pan and gently heat, stirring, to help the sugar dissolve. Add the lime zest and fruit juices and bring to the boil. Take off the heat and leave to cool. Strain and then add the rum and the Angostura bitters. Pour into an ice cream maker to churn, or a broad shallow container and freeze. If you're using the freezer, mix everything up with a fork once the liquid round the edge has started to become firm. Do this 3 or 4 times during freezing to ensure a smooth sorbet. You can put the sorbet in the food-processor and whizz it briefly instead of using a fork, but I can never be bothered with the washing up!

If you have used an ice cream machine put the sorbet into a container, cover and freeze until ready to serve.

200ml water
200g caster sugar
zest of 2 limes, removed
   with a zester
535ml grapefruit juice,
   preferably freshly squeezed
juice of 2 limes
4 tbsp light rum
a few shakes of Angostura
   bitters, or to taste

JAMAICAN SUNRISE ICE CREAM SUNDAE

SERVES 8

Here's a combination that'll get your guests licking their bowls! This will probably make more toffee sauce than you need, but keep the rest in the fridge as a delicious stand-by.

For the rum raisins
100g raisins
2 tbsp dark rum
90ml water

For the toffee sauce
200g caster sugar
60ml water
150ml double cream
150g butter, cut into
  small pieces

150ml whipping cream
4 bananas
1 litre vanilla ice cream
demarara sugar, for
  sprinkling (optional)

First make the rum raisins. Put the raisins into a small pan with the rum and water. Bring almost to the boil; turn off the heat and leave to soak for at least 20 minutes.

Meanwhile, make the toffee sauce. Put the sugar and water into a heavy-based pan and gradually dissolve the sugar over a low heat, gently drawing a spoon through it to help the process along. When the sugar has dissolved, turn up the heat and let the mixture bubble, swirling occasionally so it doesn't burn. When it has turned a caramel colour and bubbles more slowly, quickly take the pan off the heat and immediately stir in the cream and butter. Return to a low heat but don't let it boil. Leave to cool. You may need to reheat this up to pour over the ice cream later.

Shortly before you want to eat, whip the cream until it forms medium-stiff peaks. Cut the bananas into medium-thick slices.

Assemble 8 steep-sided bowls or ice cream sundae glasses and layer up each sundae with: 1 scoop ice cream, a scattering of rum-raisins, 1 spoon toffee sauce, a few banana slices, 1 scoop ice cream, 1 spoon toffee sauce, followed by the remaining banana and raisins. Top with whipped cream, a sprinkling of sugar or a little extra toffee sauce, and perhaps a couple of extra banana slices.

RUM AND CARAMEL ICE CREAM

MAKES 1 LITRE

You don't have to do your pudding on the barbecue, but it is good to have at least part of it made ahead of time. Serve this on its own or douse it in more rum or hot black coffee! I love it with barbecued fruit kebabs or Griddled Mango Cheeks (page 157).

200g sugar
90ml water
500ml full-fat milk
5 large organic egg yolks
250ml double cream
50ml dark rum
½ tsp vanilla extract

Put the sugar into a heavy-based pan with the water and heat gently. Don't stir – just gently swish the pan. When the sugar has dissolved, whack the heat up and cook until the sugar turns to caramel. You should know when this happens by the colour and smell but don't let it go too far. Pull the pan off the heat and immediately add the milk. The mixture will really splutter, so stand back. When the bubbling has subsided, stir to dissolve and return the pan to the heat to warm through. Keep stirring the caramel.

Put the egg yolks into a bowl and gently whisk. Gradually add some of the warm caramel milk, whisking as you do, then pour the egg mixture into the pan of caramel milk. Set this over a very low heat and stir continuously until the mixture is thick enough to coat the back of a spoon. Don't let it boil or it will curdle. Sit a bowl in a sink of ice-cold water. As soon as the custard is thick enough, pour it into the chilled bowl. Gently stir until cool.

Whip the cream until it just starts to hold its shape and then mix this into the cool custard. Add the rum and vanilla. Chill and then churn in an ice cream machine following the manufacturer's instructions. If you don't have an ice cream machine, place in a freezer-proof lidded container, freeze for 1½ hours and then take it out and beat by hand or in a food-processor. Do this about 4 times over 6–8 hours.

MINTY PINEAPPLE REFRESHER

SERVES 6

This is very simple, but very good. You need to add the sugar at the last minute so that it's nice and crunchy as you eat it.

Put the pineapple into a bowl with the rum, lime juice, lime zest and half the sugar. Gently turn the fruit over to coat. Cover and chill in the coldest part of the fridge for about 30 minutes. Stir in the mint and then sprinkle over the remaining sugar just before serving.

1 large ripe pineapple,
    peeled, cored and cut
    into chunks
90ml light rum
juice of 2 limes
zest of 2 limes, removed
    with a zester
100g sugar
roughly chopped leaves from
    1 bunch of fresh mint

LEVI'S JUICY JELLIES
SERVES 8

These wibbly wobblers are a really refreshing way to cleanse your palate at the end of a barbecue. Here I've chosen to use my drinks, but you can use whatever takes your fancy, adding lime juice and sugar to taste. You need to allow at least four hours for the jellies to set, but they're best made the day before serving.

12 gelatine leaves, 20g in total
400ml each Levi Roots
    Caribbean Crush; Orange,
    Papaya 'n' Lime Juice Drink;
    Blood Orange 'n' Pomegranate
    Juice Drink or other fruit
    juices, as desired
2 tbsp fresh lime juice
1 tbsp soft brown sugar

Soak the gelatine leaves in a little cold water for 5 minutes. Meanwhile, pour the drinks into separate small pans, or cook one after the other in the same pan. Stir 1 tablespoon of the lime juice into both the Caribbean Crush and the Blood Orange 'n' Pomegranate Juice Drink. Stir the sugar into the Blood Orange and Pomegranate Juice Drink. Gently heat each pan to just below boiling, and then turn off the heat.

Remove the gelatine from the water and add 4 leaves to each of the 3 pans. Carefully stir the gelatine into the liquid until dissolved.

Pour the liquid into moulds using 3 x 400ml moulds or bowls. Alternatively, use lots of small moulds (8 x 150ml moulds work well) if you want to create a wobbling display of beautiful juicy jellies on a big serving platter. Allow the jellies to cool and then chill for at least 4 hours before serving.

To unmould the jellies, dip the bases of the moulds briefly in very hot water. Put a plate on top of the mould and quickly turn over, giving a tap to help it.

MIXED MELONS IN RUM PUNCH SYRUP

SERVES 6-8

I'm a big melon lover – it's so Caribbean and so thirst-quenching. This recipe makes good syrup – you can use it for an exotic fruit salad or even summer berries. Just prepare the fruit, pour over the syrup and serve. Do try to include watermelon in your melon mix.

For the syrup
150ml water
150ml pineapple juice
200g caster sugar
2 strips of lime rind
juice of 2 limes
½ cinnamon stick
3cm piece of fresh root
  ginger, peeled and sliced
150ml white rum

800g mixed melon flesh
  (such as honeydew,
  charentais, ogen and
  watermelon), seeded
  and cubed

Put the water, pineapple juice, sugar, lime rind, lime juice, cinnamon stick and ginger into a pan and bring to the boil, stirring a little to help the sugar dissolve. Turn the heat down and simmer for about 15 minutes. You should end up with about 300ml of syrup. Pull the pan off the heat, leave to cool completely and then strain. Add the rum.

Put the melon into a large dish, pour over the syrup and chill for 20 minutes or so – you can put the cinnamon stick back in with the fruit if you want to but not the lime rind or ginger. It's best not to leave the fruit for longer than 30 minutes or so before serving, as it gets too soft.

8
DRINKs

BRING ME SUNSHINE SMOOTHIE

MAKES 1 LITRE

Sometimes the British summer isn't quite as sunshiny as we'd all like – but you can still drink smoothies made from sweet, colourful fruits and feel some Caribbean good times in your body and soul!

200g mango flesh
200g melon flesh
200g strawberries, hulled
400ml orange or pineapple juice
juice of 1 lime, or to taste

Whizz everything except the lime juice in a blender. Stir in as much lime juice as you fancy. That's it!

MANGO AND GINGER BEER ICE CREAM SODA

SERVES 1

This isn't so much a refreshing drink as a luscious liquid pudding. Mango purée can be found in some shops and is a great ingredient. If you can't find it, whizz some tinned or fresh mango in the blender with a little syrup from the tin, or water.

100ml mango purée
1 scoop vanilla ice cream
120–150ml Levi Roots
  Fiery Ginger Beer with
  Lime 'n' Honey or
  another good-quality
  fiery ginger beer
freshly grated nutmeg, to taste

Spoon the purée into a tall glass. Top with a scoop of ice cream and pour over the ginger beer. Stir, sprinkle over some nutmeg and serve with a spoon so you can eat the ice cream.

MANGO MILKSHAKE

SERVES 1

This one's for the kids, although you'll probably find the grown-ups want a glass too. You can use this recipe as the basis for other milkshakes with different fruit. Just replace the mango with berries or other ripe stone fruits. Apple juice is better with berries, orange juice with stone fruits. The recipe for the sugar syrup makes more than you need for 1 drink but it's crazy to make a tiny batch. It will keep in the fridge, covered, for your next round of milkshakes.

For the syrup, put the sugar and water in a pan and gently heat, stirring from time to time. When the sugar has dissolved, turn the heat up and boil for about 4 minutes. Leave to cool completely.

Scoop the flesh out of the mango, chop and then place in a blender. Add the other milkshake ingredients, including the ice cubes and blend. Pour into a tall glass and serve.

For the sugar syrup
250g caster sugar
250ml water

For the milkshake
½ mango, stone removed
50ml milk
1 scoop vanilla ice cream
35ml sugar syrup
25ml orange juice
a handful of ice cubes

PINA COLADA SMOOTHIE
SERVES 6

1 medium pineapple
500ml natural bio yoghurt
1 x 400g tin coconut milk
1 tsp grated nutmeg
sugar, to taste (optional)
ice, to serve

You need to make this just before serving or it goes bitter. Minus the rum, it's a refreshing and healthy take on a classic cocktail.

Peel the pineapple and cut it lengthways into quarters. Cut out the tough core and slice the flesh into chunks.

Put the pineapple into a blender with the bio yoghurt, coconut milk and nutmeg. Whizz until smooth. Taste and add some sugar if you like. Pour into glasses over ice and serve – with or without a cocktail umbrella!

BANANA DAQUIRI
SERVES 2

This is slightly less sweet than a traditional banana daquiri because of the lime juice kick. If you want it even less sweet, just adjust the sugar accordingly.

Place everything a blender and whizz. Pour into 2 cocktail glasses and serve. Simple as that!

50ml white rum
2 bananas
1 tbsp triple sec
1½ tbsp caster sugar
75ml orange juice
juice of 1 lime
a handful of ice cubes

JAMAICAN ME CRAZY
SERVES 2

This is a classic and it won't make you crazy – just chilled! Use the cap of the rum bottle as a measure.

1 measure white rum
1 measure Malibu
1 measure banana liqueur
1 measure pineapple juice
1 measure cranberry juice
a good squeeze of lime
a handful of ice, plus
  more to serve
1 fresh mint sprig, to serve

Shake the ingredients except the mint together and then pour over ice. Decorate with the mint sprig and serve immediately.

JAMAICAN MARTINI

SERVES 2-3

This might sound a bit odd – red wine in a Jamaican drink? – but it works. Plus, it's a great colour. I find the original martini slightly too dry so I have added a little Curaçao. If you can't find orange bitters just use regular bitters. Use the cap of the gin bottle as a measure.

3 measures gin
½ measure red wine
½ measure Curaçao
1 tbsp light rum
4 dashes orange bitters
a handful of ice

Put everything into a cocktail shaker, shake and serve. Don't drink too many before barbecuing – but you can have plenty once it's done!

MY GINGER EXPLOSION

MAKES 1 LITRE

My ginger beer. And then some. Don't plan on going anywhere after an evening of drinking this. It's almost too good!

For the syrup
175ml water
150g soft light brown sugar
leaves from 1 small bunch
  of fresh mint
3cm cube fresh root
  ginger, peeled
1 small chilli, halved
  and seeded
zest of 2 limes, removed
  with a knife

500ml Levi Roots Fiery
  Ginger Beer with
  Lime 'n' Honey or
  another good-quality
  fiery ginger beer
juice of 4 limes
150ml light or dark rum
4 tbsp Cointreau
a good dash of Angostura bitters
ice, fresh mint leaves and lime
  slices, (optional) to serve

To make the syrup, put the water and sugar into a pan and heat gently, stirring a little to help the sugar dissolve. Add the mint, ginger, chilli and lime zest and boil for 5 minutes. Remove from the heat, leave to cool completely and then strain.

Mix the ginger beer with the remaining ingredients and add as much of the syrup as you want. Serve over ice with more mint and lime slices.

9
RELISHES, ETC

JAMAiCAN TERiYAKi MARiNADE

MAKES ENOUGH FOR 6 SALMON STEAKS OR CHICKEN BREASTS

I've given this classic sauce an island twist by adding some refreshing orange to the mix. This is a great marinade to have ready in the fridge to make a real difference to your barbecue.

100ml Japanese soy sauce
150ml sherry
2 tbsp caster sugar
juice of 2 oranges

Put all the ingredients into a small pan, slowly bring to the boil and cook for 5 minutes, or until slightly thickened. Leave to cool.

Marinate meaty fish such as salmon, cod or tuna for 15 minutes, then barbecue. Alternatively, marinate chicken breasts for a couple of hours.

While the meat or fish is cooking, return the marinade to the pan and boil for another 5 minutes until slightly syrupy. Pour a little over the barbecued goodies at the end, perhaps with a scattering of sesame seeds and some finely chopped spring onion.

ALL-PURPOSE SEASONING RUB

MAKES ENOUGH FOR 24 PORTIONS OF JERK CHICKEN, STEAKS OR CHOPS

In Jamaican kitchens you often see a pot of seasoning. It's one of the big bustas of the kitchen. On my food and music tours, I bring out the pestle and mortar between songs and do a seasoning rub like this after performing my first hit, Jahovia. Well, here's how to make your own. Play around with different spices to get your own home-brand. Rub it onto chicken, pork, lamb, fish or veggie burgers to give them that extra lift.

Put everything except the salt and chilli powder into a spice grinder, or use a pestle and mortar. Grind to a medium-fine texture. Transfer to a small bowl and mix with salt and chilli powder, to taste.

3 tbsp black peppercorns
1½ tbsp allspice berries
2 tbsp coriander seeds
2 tsp grated nutmeg
3 tsp dried thyme
½–1 tsp salt
1–2 tsp chilli powder, optional

PINEAPPLE AND RUM MARINADE

MAKES ENOUGH FOR 10 CHICKEN PIECES OR LAMB CHOPS, OR 15 SAUSAGES

When it comes to Caribbean food, pineapple and rum have to be two of the tops. So here they are, joined together in happy matrimony in one beautiful marinade-glaze. This is great with chicken, pork or even lamb or beef – not only is the flavour great, but the pineapple juice works to tenderise meat nicely.

500ml pineapple juice
100ml dark rum
1 tbsp finely grated
   fresh root ginger
2 tbsp soft light
   brown sugar
12 allspice berries,
   lightly crushed

Put everything into a pan and slowly heat to dissolve the sugar. Increase the heat and boil for 5 minutes to reduce slightly. Set aside to cool.

Use this mixture as a marinade for your chicken or meat – you want to let it absorb all the flavours for a couple of hours if possible. Remove the meat or chicken from the marinade, shaking off any excess, and place on the barbecue. While the food is cooking, return the marinade to the pan and bring to the boil. Reduce to a sticky glaze and brush this over the chicken or meat towards the end of cooking to give a final layer of flavour and a beautiful shine.

FRUITY SCOTCH BONNET SALSA
SERVES 6

170g pineapple,
  cut into 1cm dice
220g mango flesh,
  cut into 1cm dice
1 red onion, peeled
  and finely diced
½ Scotch Bonnet, or
  other hot chilli, seeded
  and very finely chopped
½ tsp fine salt
a big squeeze of lime
2 tbsp finely chopped
  fresh coriander

Here's a great all-purpose fresh salsa that goes well with anything – sausages, hamburgers, veggie burgers or roasted peppers. The secret lies in the balance between the sweet fruit, the hot chilli, the salt and the sharp lime juice. The Scotch Bonnet is the hot Jamaican chilli, with a fruity taste and aroma of its own that works brilliantly with tropical fruit.

Mix everything together really well shortly before serving – ideally no longer than 30 minutes – to get the very best of the fresh flavours.

PICKLED PINEAPPLE
SERVES 4

250ml cider vinegar
100ml apple juice
350g sugar
1 cinnamon stick, broken in half
1 tsp allspice berries
2 slices fresh root ginger,
  about 3mm thick
2 tsp chilli flakes
1 pineapple, peeled, cored and
  cut into bite-sized chunks

This works brilliantly with Soy-Griddled Tuna (page 94), as well as plain barbecued pork and chicken.

Put all the ingredients except the pineapple itself, into a non-reactive pan and bring to the boil. Stir a little to help dissolve the sugar. Reduce the heat, add the pineapple and simmer for about 15 minutes. At the end of cooking the pineapple should still be covered in liquid. Remove from the heat and leave to cool to room temperature. Chill for 24 hours before serving, to improve the flavour.

CUCUMBER, AVOCADO AND MINT RELISH

SERVES 4-6

A cool number! Serve with tortilla chips or other 'dippers' while you're waiting for the barbecue to get going. Or eat it with barbied fish – it's brilliant with the Salmon Baked in Newspaper (page 87).

½ cucumber
4 tbsp rice vinegar
½ tbsp caster sugar
1 tbsp groundnut oil
1 avocado
1 red chilli, seeded and
  finely sliced
2 tbsp chopped fresh mint
salt and pepper

Halve the cucumber lengthways and scoop out the seeds with a teaspoon. Slice very finely and set aside in a bowl.

To make the dressing, mix the rice vinegar and sugar together stirring to help the sugar dissolve. Add the groundnut oil and salt and pepper.

Halve the avocado and remove the stone. Cut each half into slices and peel each slice. Cut the avocado flesh into small cubes and add to the cucumber with the dressing. The avocado needs to be dressed immediately or it will go brown.

Add the chilli and mint to the cucumber and avocado, and gently toss everything together. Don't make this too far in advance – no more than a couple of hours – or it will completely lose its freshness.

HOT PINEAPPLE CHUTNEY
FiLLS 2 X 500ML JARS

You should try to make this well in advance of your barbecue because chutney improves with age. You'll need to sterilize two jam jars. Just wash the jars and their lids and heat in a 170°C/325°F/Gas 3 oven for about 20 minutes. Very carefully pot the chutney while the jars are still hot. If you're going to eat all the chutney soon after cooking, there's no need to sterilize the jars.

Heat the oil in a large heavy-based pan and sauté the onions until soft but not coloured. Add the chillies, ginger and allspice and sauté for another minute, then add the pineapple, lime zest and the juice of 2 limes. Stir and add the vinegar. Bring to the boil, immediately turn the heat down and cook for 30 minutes. When the pineapple is tender, stir in the sugar and simmer for 30–45 minutes more. The mixture should be thick – if you scrape a spoon across the bottom of the pan it should leave a channel for a few seconds before it fills up again. Add the remaining lime juice for some final freshness and zing.

While the chutney is still warm, pot it in hot sterilized jars and cover with vinegar-proof lids. Don't forget to label your jars! Leave for a few days – it will get better if you can leave it a couple of weeks – before serving it at your barbecue. It goes brilliantly with pork.

2 tbsp groundnut oil
2 red onions, peeled
   and roughly chopped
2 red and 1 green chilli,
   seeded and finely sliced
2cm cube fresh ginger
   root, peeled and grated
1 tsp crushed allspice
2 pineapples, peeled, cored
   and cut into small chunks
grated zest and juice of
   3 limes
175ml cider vinegar
250g soft light brown sugar

SWEET ONION, TOMATO AND CHILLI SAUCE
SERVES 8

You can make this sauce in advance and bring it out to add some Caribbean magic to burgers, bangers, chicken, steak, fish, roasted vegetables – anything!

1 tbsp olive oil
3 large onions, peeled and
   finely sliced
2 garlic cloves, finely chopped
pinch of soft light brown
   sugar, or to taste
salt
6 tomatoes, roughly chopped
½ Scotch Bonnet or other
   hot chilli, seeded and
   finely chopped

Heat the oil in a large heavy-based pan over a medium-low heat and add the onions and garlic. Sprinkle over the sugar and season well with salt. Cook for 10 minutes, stirring occasionally so the onions don't catch on the bottom of the pan and burn. Turn down the heat and continue to cook for 20–30 minutes, or until soft, melting and sweet.

Add the tomatoes, turn up the heat slightly and continue to cook for 20 minutes, stirring occasionally. Add the chilli 10 minutes before the end. Taste and adjust the seasoning with more sugar or salt.

Keep in the fridge, covered, until needed – it's best eaten within 1 week.

SMOKED CHILLI MAYO

SERVES 8

Smoke doesn't just come from the barbecue, it comes from spices too, and the chipotle – dried ancho chilli – is one of the best places to get it. This is fabulicious with barbied prawns and will keep in the fridge for a couple of days.

Toast the chillies in a dry frying pan for about 3 minutes – they should start to curl slightly. Tip them into a small pan and cover with water. Simmer for about 15 minutes until soft and then drain and remove the stalks. Put the chillies into a mortar with the salt and grind to a paste. Set aside.

Put the egg yolks into a bowl and stir in the Dijon mustard, salt and pepper and about 1 tablespoon of lime juice. Mix the oils together in a jug and start adding them 1 drop at a time to the egg yolks while beating vigorously. I do mean 1 drop at a time! Use a wooden spoon or an electric whisk, and always incorporate the last lot of oil before you add more. When the mixture starts to thicken and look like mayonnaise you can add the oil in a larger quantity, but be careful not to add too much too quickly or it will split. You may not need all the oil.

Add the chilli paste, hot sauce and paprika. Taste and add more lime juice if you like and adjust the seasoning – you need to balance the richness and the citrus. Add the warm water and stir. When you are happy with the taste, cover with clingfilm. Stir vigorously before serving.

6 dried chipotle chillis
pinch of sea salt flakes
2 organic egg yolks
1 tsp Dijon mustard
3–4 tbsp lime juice
150ml olive oil
150ml sunflower oil
1 tbsp X Hot Reggae Reggae
   Sauce or hot chilli sauce
1–2 tsp smoked paprika
½ tbsp warm water
salt and pepper

RELISHES, ETC

BANANA KETCHUP
MAKES ABOUT 300ML

Banana ketchup is a delicious condiment popular in the Caribbean. This fresh version is slightly less sweet than the commercial kind and a really interesting partner for chicken and pork. Away from the barbecue, some of you may like a dollop of this in a bacon butty!

1 x 400g tin tomatoes
  or 400g fresh tomatoes
1½ ripe medium bananas,
  peeled and sliced
30g fresh root ginger,
  peeled and chopped
1–2 garlic cloves, finely chopped
½ Scotch Bonnet or other
  hot red chilli, seeded
  and finely chopped
2 tsp fresh thyme leaves
1 tsp finely grated nutmeg
1 tsp ground allspice
5 tbsp soft dark brown sugar
2 tsp salt
3 tbsp cider vinegar
1 cinnamon stick

Put all the ingredients except the cinnamon in a blender and whizz until smooth, scraping down the sides of the jug if necessary. If you're worried about heat, add half the chilli first, taste and add more depending on how hot you want your ketchup.

Pour the mixture into a pan and simmer for 20–30 minutes, stirring occasionally, especially at the end of cooking to ensure the sauce doesn't catch on the bottom of the pan. Taste and adjust the seasoning if necessary, adding more vinegar, sugar, salt and chilli to taste.

Remove the cinnamon stick and pour the sauce into a clean, lidded jar. This will keep in the fridge for about 1 week.

MY HOT MUSTARD

MAKES ABOUT 125ML

Wow, this is hot, hot, hot, so be careful! It's
fab with sausages – of course – and also with
burgers, steak and pork chops.

100ml Dijon or grain mustard
1 tbsp soft dark brown sugar
¼ tsp chilli powder, or to taste
1 tsp English mustard
1 tbsp X Hot Reggae Reggae
   Sauce or hot chilli sauce
juice of ½ lime
½ tbsp dark rum

Simply mix all the ingredients together and chill.
Just take it out of the fridge and bring it back to
room temperature before you use it.

INDEX

I'd like to thank my Mum, my children (Jo-anne, Danai, Zaion, Sharlene, Bernice, Natalie and Tyran), Laura Herring and Carey Smith from Ebury Publishing, Diana Henry and Hattie Ellis, Sara and Andrew Lewis, Martin Poole for his photography, Alex and all at Smith & Gilmour for their design and art direction, Tamzin Ferdinando for the brilliant styling, Giles and Sarah Kane, James and Susie Adam, Shah Khan and Tim Beard, Teja Picton Howell, John Eastaff, Jake Brocklehurst, Rodney Levine Boateng and Natasha Eggough, Borra Garson and Emma Hughes.

I'd also like to give a big mention to Mrs Pots from the St Lucia Coalpot Company for my beautiful coalpot. www.stluciacoalpot.co.uk